Contents

For my mother and father

Acknowledgements

My students past and present who devised theatre and in so doing helped make this book.

For time, production material and being inspiring, Toby Wilsher of Trestle Theatre, Phelim McDermott and Lee Simpson of Improbable Theatre, Alan Lyddiard of The Northern Stage Ensemble, Michèle Young of Passe-Partout, Peter Ellis, Sue Gibbons and Anita Parry.

For material from *Suffering and the Supreme Being*, the students who laboured in its creation, particularly Rowena Deletant and Faye Hunter. For advice on *The Rise of Physical Theatre*, George Dillon. For discussing ideas, reading and commenting on drafts and unquestioning enthusiasm and belief in the project, Lisa Peck. For helping in more ways than I can say, my sister Celia. For support at Hodder, Kate Mayhew, Caroline Marriage and Kate Harrison.

For being there and making me laugh, my children Boris and Madeleine, and most important for making time, tea and giving invaluable advice, Adam.

Introduction

Why Make Theatre?

Drama students are continually making and creating touching, exciting, daring theatre pieces which hold and inspire their audiences. Watching students make and perform reminds me why we need drama: it is a creative art. Making and watching it frees us from the banalities of everyday life and lifts us into a world of imagination where anything is possible. Drama communicates a different sort of truth and this truth connects us to each other and to society on a deeper level than most exchanges of everyday life allow. At its best it is risk taking; it is passion; it is commitment. Worthwhile theatre extends our perceptions of ourselves, others and the possibilities of the world we live in. It enriches and nourishes us and moves us on.

Devised versus Scripted Work

Devised and script-led theatre both share the capacity to move on the audience, but there are clear differences between them. Script-led theatre is fundamentally literary. A text is the starting point which is interpreted in rehearsal by a group of actors and a director. The essence of devised theatre is a group of people working and rehearsing together over a period of time to create a performance text. Its excitement and challenge is the freedom to bring ideas, creativity, knowledge, exploration of dramatic form and the unique dynamic of a group of people working together to create a production, which is an expression of a group of people's views on their topic at a particular moment in time.

Implicit in devising is the notion of ephemerality. Without a text or documentation, it is difficult to ascribe a value to the theatre piece. It cannot be placed in a canon of established, revered work. Perhaps this is why devised theatre tends to carry a lower status in society than traditional theatre.

Why devise?

You are at the thresholds of your lives; you live, you experience, you care. You uniquely experience life as it is, and have the passion and energy to communicate it. You are in a position to control your own learning, and have freedom to produce a piece of theatre for an audience about a topic that concerns you. You have a platform and are artists. As artists you will respond to your environment and experiences, things you have seen and heard which have impacted on your life. All artists reflect aspects of themselves in their work. That is what makes it unique.

The furthest most students in other subjects go, no matter how brilliant their ideas, is to a teacher, moderator or examiner. You perform to an audience. This is scary and exciting. You need to make sure that what you say is important to you, will engage your audience, and that you have access to the tools that enable you to say it in the most dynamic and effective way.

Focusing in

Devising theatre, as opposed to writing theatre, is becoming increasingly popular as a form. Some of our most exciting contemporary performances arise from a devising process. It is also embedded in Drama education through GCSE to degree level. Exam specifications give high status to the devising process, recognising its importance in contemporary theatre and in terms of the learning curve actor-students ascend in the process of devising.

This manual shows you how to devise in a way that fulfils potential. It shows it is not an easy option: you'll work harder on devised pieces than on almost anything else in your course. If you are open to the process, you will make discoveries about performance, creativity, the nature of collaboration and much more. The emphasis is on practical work, practical advice, examples, tasks and a structured framework which will enable you to devise and thrive.

Using the text

The text is addressed to you as an active participant. A staggered approach to chapters 1–5 may be most appropriate. Chapters 1–3 lay

Devising:
A Handbook for Drama and Theatre Students

Gill Lamden

Hodder & Stoughton

A MEMBER OF THE HODDER HEADLINE GROUP

Copyright Photographs:
p22, © Trestle Theatre Company; p34, © Improbable Theatre/Shelia Barnett; p38, © Julian Crouch; p46, © Keith Pattison; p53, © Bob Curtis Photography.

Copyright Text:
pp114–5 Extract from *Engineers of the Imagination: The Welfare State Handbook* by Tony Coult and Baz Kershaw, Methuen, 1990.

Orders: please contact Bookpoint Ltd, 78 Milton Park, Abingdon, Oxon OX14 4TD. Telephone: (44) 01235 827720, Fax: (44) 01235 400454. Lines are open 9.00a.m.–6.00p.m., Monday to Saturday, with a 24-hour message answering service. Email address: *orders@bookpoint.co.uk*

British Library Cataloguing in Publication Data
A catalogue record for this title is available from The British Library

ISBN 0 340 78008 8

First published   2000
Impression number   10 9 8 7 6 5 4 3 2
Year   2005 2004 2003 2002 2001 2000

Copyright © 2000 Gill Lamden

Cover photo © Donald Cooper/Photostage
Typeset by Multiplex Techniques Ltd, Brook Industrial Park, Mill Brook Road, St. Mary Cray, Kent BR5 3SR
Printed in Great Britain for Hodder & Stoughton Educational, a division of Hodder Headline Plc, 338 Euston Road, London NW1 3BH by Redwood Books Ltd, Trowbridge, Wiltshire.

the groundwork. Chapters 4 and 5 engage you in the practice. Try to work on them some weeks before devising your own piece of theatre. It takes time to assimilate ideas and practice. Chapters 6–8 speak for themselves and apply most directly to the process of devising. Learning areas are summarised at the start of each chapter. Chapters end with summative statements followed by questions addressed to you as devisers. Questions within the text are in *italics*. Throughout there are statements making explicit points.

Chapters 1–3 share practice. Engage with them independently and follow up practical work in groups. The act of writing clarifies thinking. Get a journal to use alongside the text. Note good ideas and good practice, also what touches and inspires you. Devising is about working collaboratively and chapters 4 and 5 reflect this. Activities are workshop based. Words in *italics* that may be unfamiliar are explained in the Glossary.

Success in devising (as in many things) is a matter of self-belief, and the discipline to acquire and develop appropriate knowledge and skills. Work carefully and systematically through this manual and you will be surprised how quickly your understanding of the practice develops.

The tutor examiner

The tutor is in place because they have expert knowledge and understanding of drama. They know more than you. They want you to fulfil your potential and will support you in the process. It is important that the devised piece is owned by the devising students, so you need to be clear exactly how and when you want your tutor to advise and support you. You stay in control.

Your tutor may also be your examiner, which can be confusing. A group I once worked with was in difficulty, yet kept refusing help. Eventually one of the students explained that, as examiner, I needed to be surprised and impressed on the day. In seeing me as examiner, he had forgotten my role as expert! During the process, treat your tutor as an expert and call on them for advice; by the exam they will have a clear idea of your motivation and input and will see you in your best light.

1 The Rise of Physical Theatre

In professional theatre, there are a number of companies committed to devising who have worked together for some years. For example Red Ladder (founded 1968) is a socialist, feminist collective whose brief is to take to young people artistically stimulating work which forces them to ask questions. Trestle Theatre (founded 1981) is a mask-based company whose aim is to integrate mask into the popular theatre. Greenwich Young People's Theatre Company (founded 1970) provides a professional theatre-in-education service for schools in South East London. The longer established companies have particular skills and briefs which they promote through their performances. They almost invariably tour to small-scale modern theatres or Arts Centres and their appeal is likely to be to a younger age-group than is traditional for West End theatre. The styles and devices they use will depend on their particular skills. Forkbeard Fantasy – The Brittonioni Brothers combine live performance with cinematic techniques in bizarre and comic shows, whereas Age Exchange specialise in reminiscence pieces for the elderly.

The 1960s and 1970s saw the formation of many devising companies working in a range of different genres. *Mike Alfreds* (Shared Experience) and *Mike Leigh* (*Abigail's Party*, *Secrets and Lies*, etc.) were recently out of drama school and developing skills in naturalistic devising with an episodic narrative. Welfare State was developing street extravaganzas in the community in a celebration of popular culture. 7:84 also drew on popular theatre forms with a highly political agenda.

At the same time *Steven Berkoff* was writing, directing and performing a new style of theatre which he called '*total*' or '*non-concept*' theatre. Plays like *Metamorphosis* and *East* caught the imagination of a generation and started to radicalise textual performance. Word, action, light, and sound had equal status in plays that were always exciting, energetic and often confrontational. Berkoff paved the way for the next generation of performers.

In the late 1970s and early 1980s a new genre emerged which was ideally suited to devising companies; *Physical Theatre* emanating particularly from the Jacques Lecoq School, Paris. It was popularised in the work of Theatre de Complicite. Their earliest plays like *A Minute Too Late* and *More Bigger Snacks Now* brought a different kind of show to the stage.

Productions were based on physical skill. The meaning was played very vividly through actions rather than through a coherent narrative. Actors became objects, and seemed infinitely flexible in the variety of objects they could become. The pieces were absurd yet curiously accurate observations of life. They were surprising, entertaining and capable of moving the audience to tears of pain and laughter. They told fantastical stories which reached deep into the imaginations of the audience. The work was new and exciting, and drew in enthusiastic young audiences. Theatre was freed from epic and naturalistic forms, but the style was difficult to access for students not trained in movement.

One advantage of text-based plays over devised is they can be published. Berkoff's *Metamorphosis* has been in print since 1978. What was remarkable in the production – which is the transformation of Kafka's nightmare into tangible reality – was also remarkable in the text. Berkoff had written the rubric for a complete physical performance text. His intention in publishing the text was to describe his production; however, that description and the text of *East* also came to function as a training ground for students and young actors interested in exploring how to move away from naturalistic styles. In the action described, it was possible for those who knew little about mime to discover how meaning could be articulated physically. Berkoff had started to provide a vocabulary for physical theatre.

In the late 1980s, Theatre de Complicite and Steven Berkoff continued to pioneer the way for physically based pieces crossing the boundary from fringe to mainstream with text-based plays. In 1989 Complicite played *The Visit* at The National Theatre while Berkoff directed and acted in *Salome.*

Other companies like *The Northern Stage Ensemble, Trestle Theatre, The David Glass Mime Ensemble* and *Volcano Theatre* also conveyed their meaning largely through visual and poetic images. They brought to the stage a new theatre vocabulary, achieving meaning through a combination of movement, text, design and lighting. Although each show had a director, the content was discovered through a physically led rehearsal process designed to free the creative self through play. Complicitè, under Arden and McBurney's direction, have made a significant impact on our collective understanding of theatre.

On the cusp of the millennium a new wave of written text is emerging whose fractured narrative explores taboos of sex and violence in productions like Northern Stage's *Clockwork Orange*, Sarah Keane's *Blasted* and Mark Ravenhill's *Shopping and F***ing*. One writer, Alex Sierz, called the style 'in yer face' because of the explicit nature of the violence and sex depicted on stage. I suspect there is a relationship between these plays, the rise of Physical Theatre and young people devising on Drama courses. What impact on theatre will your generation be making ten years from now?

In Physical Theatre there is freedom to explore and create physically, rather than a dependence on the quality of the writing. It draws on a broader range of skills than text-based theatre, and as its forms and devices are drawn from so many places, it can say virtually anything.

Seeing devised theatre

There is no substitute for seeing live theatre. The images will stay with you and inform your practice more than you can imagine. Most devising companies tour the length and breadth of the UK. If you live far away from cities and towns on the touring circuit, the Edinburgh Fringe Festival each August is an excellent opportunity to see a lot of exciting devised theatre. Most devising companies began their theatrical life there. You could take your own play...

▶ **Start thinking about your own devising.**

▶ **Consider what theatre forms excite you, and which you would like to explore in the devising process. Keep asking yourself this question.**

2 Actors on Devising

The chapter presents interviews with theatre practitioners who have a particular interest in devising:

- Sue Gibbons talks about young people and the process of devising;
- Peter Ellis considers approaches to character creation; and
- Anita Parry talks about techniques for making a play.

Sue Gibbons: Young People and the Work of Devising

> 'Young people's heads are so full of passions and hatreds, and new ideas and new realisations.'

Sue Gibbons has worked as director, actor and teacher. She is now a freelance director and facilitates Drama and Theatre Master Classes. She has worked extensively with young people on scripted and devised performances. In this interview she explores the nature of the devising experience for young people, considering

- devising as discovery;
- devising as empowerment; and
- devising in a group.

The special nature of devising

Devising is a forum for devisers to explore something that matters, and say it in their own language using their own words. In performance they are given a hearing. The level at which they communicate their message is in their control. Devising is to do with discovery of self, others, drama and theatre in relation to the world; of how you can bring about change however small, how you can raise other people's awareness as well as your own. I've always thought it's the most wonderful world to work in because you touch so many other worlds. One moment investigating homelessness, maybe for the first time for some people, the next exploring something wonderfully strange about a small community living in India. Your whole being is submerged in that world. It's about ownership, negotiation, compromise, developing and exploring feelings, ideas, and philosophies. It's about spontaneity, excitement, and originality. It's about the dynamics and chemistry of this group of people at this moment in time, which changes from day to day – one person perhaps becomes uncooperative, or another person is feeling low.

Additionally, and what people largely don't understand, are the skills students learn as a result of devising. The very act of working together, the unity of purpose through which you move towards a performance, is so rare. If I ask, 'What have you valued most?', they'll say 'I've learnt diplomacy, compromise, getting my own way, to be sensitive, to be generous, to deal with people, to organise, to manage to work to a real deadline.' The skills developed by devisers are those valued by management trainers. There's no bullshit on performance. You can't say, 'I've left my performance on my bed', 'My mum tidied my room', 'The cat was sick on it'. The performance is public, it happens at a time and you can't go back on that moment.

Assessing a range of skills

The joy of theatre is it encompasses so many arts and facilitates so many other skills. Young people, whether they are devising for love or need, from an early point must understand that the skills of designer, lighting or sound technician are as valuable as those of the actor. Their place in the team is absolute. Every group needs its members, someone inspirational, a good organiser, someone who supports a less able person. These all have potential for excellent marks. Being *the leader* isn't necessarily the key role. Some students will get better grades, that's life. Students place themselves according to their ability and their drive. Some students are inspirational. Others may need to allow that person to flourish and find their place in the group accordingly. It's about seeing your role and having the generosity to accept that. At 17 or 18 that's asking a lot.

The role of the tutor

There is something strange that suddenly at 17 you give young people a topic or opportunity and expect they will know how to make it into theatre. Their life experience doesn't teach them how. They need a support system, often emotional. The subjects that are touched on are hard. People are very fragile when experimenting and daring to push their work on. There's a lot at risk. At the moment of public showing, they're very fragile deep down. There is nothing to hide behind. It is entirely their work, and they want to own it. Their vision on stage is terribly exposing. Of course they need support and help. Adults need it, why not young devisers?

Practical support

The essence is, 'Don't tell me, show me. Translate your ideas into immediate moments of theatre'. Start with imaging. Create a physical image of the essence of the idea. The idea has become pictorial. Immediately they've created a theatrical platform from which they can move forwards. A group working on hell might image the essence of hell. Then they look without talking, for silence is very creative. Then they recall. Then they question. Then they share: who are these people? why are they there? Immediately there are ideas. The dialogue has begun. In **Forum Theatre** there is a wonderful technique called The Crystal Ball in which you recall what you remember most powerfully from the previous session. In silence, you recreate what *you* remember, *your* truth. It confirms this was a powerful image, and that is what you build on.

Young people's heads are so full of passions and hatreds, and new ideas and new realisations. There is so much in their lives they feel strongly about and disturbed by. Where do they start, because until now someone has led them there? Devisers are overwhelmed with ideas, the task feels too big. Perhaps the starting point is a poem, part of a story, or an issue. Use a structure which says 'consider your topic'; crystallise three ideas. Image those, create freeze frames, and *look*, and ask *what touches* about those images. Then develop. You can always move on. Working with images helps create an aesthetic.

Enabling creative work

I work to create a oneness of purpose, an evenness, unity and complicity within the group. There is no room for someone who is always pulling focus. Creating this unity is to do with release and enjoyment, with exercises creating trust and confidence. You create a working atmosphere in which it's OK to make a mistake. There is no right and wrong, but a better way, another way. I work physically with a lot of **trust exercises**, taking them to the stage where they can call 'Falling' and go to fall because they know the group will catch them. I value **energisers** and having fun. We always explore what we play and why. The more they hear 'that was to do with focus', or 'spatial awareness', the more they will understand about how to work.

As an actor, I acknowledge the difficulties of performance through understanding what it's like to be a performer. I don't ask people to do things I won't do. One of the most useful things I learnt at drama school is that actors are fragile; they need to be valued; they need positive indication of how they are doing; and they need to know they are getting it right in some way. Directors, tutors and co-devisers need to find a way of marking that for them.

Research develops devisers' depth of understanding of issues and topics. It is an opportunity to delve into the different worlds, to empathise in a world you weren't previously aware of. What a wasted opportunity not to research the time, the place, the period, whatever, because your approach is then only surface. Depth of research allows you to communicate with the audience on variety of levels. Your piece is layered, the complex understanding reflected through subtext, characterisation, an unexpected scene or image, or in set design or costume. You make available to the audience what you understand. If you only have one layer, that's what they'll get.

Devising involves a lot of discovery. It's important to play first, to improvise, then set it structurally. Writing implies ownership, and difficulties can be created by able writers who want to write for a devised piece. Ultimately the text emerges, and writing it gives validity. For a technical crew, the value of a written script is enormous. Now personal computers make it easy to change what's been written, so why not keep writing and changing?

Achieving potential comes through the desire to push themselves. Being clear about ground rules. Not letting people down. Letting people know if you're sick. Being honest. Being heard. Respecting others and being respected. Not being cagey about criticism, not being precious. These things are ever so adult and difficult because you're exposed. It may be difficult to put ideas forward, when you're not sure if they're workable, or to get up and improvise when you don't know what to do. You're taking a great risk – you have to trust you won't be battered. Devisers need to be empowered, respected, in a safe place, with unity of purpose, and sensitivity to others' views.

Where I start is 'learn with one another what it is that excites you'. There are many possibilities for different rehearsals: image – 'this is me today, how I'm feeling'; poems, tiny pictures, little images that touch; brainstorming issues; interest in a particular style like *naturalism* or *physical theatre*. Are you excited by a political message? What issues are close to your heart? What current events have touched you? Image or sculpt your group into an issue that's a concern for you: what excites you out of that? Draw on personal experience. Have the ideas and visions. One group did a powerful piece about breakdown in relationship and communication. All they'd done is take their parents and relationships from the idyll to the breakdown. It was based on fact. It touched them on a daily basis whether the relationship was happy or not. It was their experience at a time when their own relationships are so volatile, exciting, passionate. If people will dare tell a story, then do it.

Summary

Sue focuses on the passions and excitements that can be reflected through devising theatre. She also reminds us of how difficult the group process can be and how vitally important it is to trust and rely on the people you work with. She encourages students to explore issues and ideas which are abstract, in a physical way to generate ideas for plot and character development.

Questions

- What exercises have you experienced which might be good for building trust in a group?

- How important do you think it is to have an issue or theme for your work? Do you think you should start with an aim or message from the audience?

- What help would you seek from a tutor in your devising work and how would you retain ownership?

Peter Ellis: Approaches to Creating Character

'The great danger with devised work is an actor's instinct to create an amazing character for themselves so they appear slightly mad.'
'Devised work often has a lot of quiet in it – but actors think they have to speak.'

Peter Ellis is an actor who has worked extensively on stage, in film, on radio and TV. Amongst other things, he currently works on *The Bill*. In this interview, he talks about:

- truth and integrity in character and plot;
- challenging techniques for building characters and plot; and
- structures for character-based devised work.

A background in devising

Devising techniques have been in film a long time. The first director I worked with here was Ken Loach. He would set up an improvisation, film it, and that's it. He didn't rehearse. His view was you get an amazing edge, particularly on film. In the first improvisation, actors were most natural and real. The longer it went on the more they refined it. Actors try to protect their own personalities, and they do what they think are clever 'actory' things as well. The audience like to see what's more real. Loach will introduce people into a scene you don't know about, for example, sitting round a table, another person will join you. The effect looks very natural; the danger is that after a while actors get used to being shocked. You open a door and think 'what's going to be round the corner?' You become wary of that way of working.

There's a lot of room for devised and improvised work within the structure of the text. I've always tried to get the writer to write open scenes for devising, getting from point to point. It's quite easy in film. We did it on *The Bill* at first. The director would invite us to improvise the beginnings and ends of scenes.

The other approach was Mike Leigh's, which is almost the total reverse. It involves a tremendous amount of detailed work before actually coming to the finished thing. Mike Leigh goes to a scripted version of the improvisations. He will have individual sessions with the actor where you try and work out characters for them, usually based on somebody they know, at least that's the starting point; I suspect he's already got a fairly good idea of what he wants. You do a lot of detailed work on your own, then gradually you'll be introduced to characters within that framework.

I did a play, *First Blush,* with Sarah Anderson (currently in the USA producing *ER*). She was a subtler version of Mike Leigh. I played a northern miner who was middle-aged and out of work. I didn't know which other people would be in the play for two or three weeks. Improvisations happened in real situations. Sarah Anderson worked taking out individuals, twos or threes. We did things like going into pubs, ordering drinks, talking and being in character. It is disquieting when the director writes notes next to you. I acquired a son, then met him. I didn't have a wife. There were two other female characters, one a pianist in a local Working Men's Club, the other a young girl from Ireland. The original plan was for the couples to get together. But it didn't work out like that. This is where devised work is fascinating and slightly worrying. We all went out to a night club in Sheffield. We were in role all night. On the way back the son said something which made me *not* go with the woman, but home with him. The evening ended with a long, rather tortuous conversation with the Irish girl about what I would like to do in life. It became a very good play about people not communicating well. It was as much about silences as what people said. In a lot of devised plays I've done, actors jump in, feeling they need to say something. In real life you don't need to do that.

Methodology

You do all character work with the director – talk a lot about what your character's like. You have to agree about where the person's come from, what their attitudes are, and so on. Information is fed gently in with questions – Is he married? Has he children? Situations are partly dictated by what characters do, like spending time in the Club. You do lots and lots of improvisations, then directors pick what they want for the play. We took lots from the Club but we did improvisations in homes, out of doors and one in the pit. This arose because, when improvising, I said, 'It's an open day, do you want to come down next week?' and I saw Sarah think, 'We have to go down the pit.'

The director/actor relationship is based on trust. You don't discuss the improvisation with the director. If you're in character, the problem for the director is to accept what the actor does. They can't say, 'I didn't like you doing that', because that was the character doing it. It's not up to the actor to do objective things like liking or disliking. The problem is whether the actor is being honest. I find myself thinking, 'Is that me the character saying "I don't want to go out tonight" or me the actor?' It's difficult to know whether you as an actor are trying to push the improvisation in a way which isn't actually very truthful for the character. The extraordinary thing is you do get very inside the character. We did *First Blush* in Sheffield, and a year later we revived it at The Bush. We knew every line. The director said, 'Get into character,' and it was all there. You feel incredibly confident and solid on stage because you know who you are and what you're doing.

The ideas come from **Stanislavski**. At Drama School it was a way of getting into text, then it became an end in itself.

The future

We have to think about who art is being made for. In this country it's bound up with class issues. Philip Hendry at Stratford East is doing amazing work with a healthy dose of vulgarity. A directors' theatre is a controlled, refined event. But it has lost the edge which will make it appeal to a larger audience. Directors' views of good and bad acting aren't necessarily the same as audiences'. Theatre survived for hundreds of years without directors. It should be a collaborative journey. Too much is put on directors; the best are those that let actors come up with ideas. Audiences like to be surprised. Devised work can bring a surprising truth, freshness and vulnerability to performance. As the arts become less accessible, audiences are pushed into passive roles. For a healthy theatrical life, we should be doing it and watching it.

Developing technology is also impacting on theatre and drama form. Digital technology has made filming cheap and immediate. It has an effect on an audience. People believe it's real. Visual images on stage can be very effective. For instance doing a drama about World War 1 with 15- and 16-year-old boys, I filmed the boys outside, in costume, as though they were at war in France. It centred the whole piece. They were the same age as boys who were killed. The glamour went. It brings another environment into theatre. It is instant, done, finished and you play it back on the TV screen or projector.

Summary

Peter Ellis has a broad experience of using improvisation in film. The potential for creating characters through spontaneous improvisation, then allowing the characters themselves to create a plot, is something which might influence your work. In Peter's experience the director relies on the actor to generate material and then shapes it, breaking down the traditional actor/director relationship.

Questions

- How important is it to create strong and honest characters? How might you do this? (See also pp. 116–117, on Stanislavski; and p. 119, on Trestle Theatre's '**tension states**'.

- How might you use digital technology in your work?

- Is going out in role a valid way of developing character? How might you strive for truth in your own work?

Anita Parry: Some Devising Techniques

'It was very workmanlike and better for it.'
'Be grounded in truth.'

Anita Parry is Co-Artistic Director of Theatre and Beyond, a Company dedicated to new and innovative forms of theatre. She is also an actor and director who has worked in professional and community theatre. In this interview, she recalls the creation of a devised piece at East 15 Drama School and shares thoughts on creating character. East 15's approach to training is Stanislavski-based, i.e. it is concerned to train actors in a system that will enable them to present truthful characters in performance.

Our Third Year production, a culmination of all our **Stanislavski** experience, was devised. We had become an ensemble over the course, and though not all were brilliant actors, everyone was strengthened by it. We had learnt to listen and be generous. The piece was devised in East 15's Yorkshire house, Sheriff Hutton, over one term. The director asked us to choose a random character, one we would really like to play. Initially we worked on a monologue or defining moment and chose a room to be in for making her public – the character grew out of this simple task. I had always wanted to play a Liverpudlian; I christened her Jessica and decided to give her an obsession and quite coldbloodedly started dressing the mannequin/character. I designed her to reflect her obsessive, dippy nature. After a week of working alone, I made my home in the beautiful library which was at odds with my character. Why would she be there? When the director came, I did an improvisation based on her desires, a wish list. Jessica wanted a child and to be close to her husband. The director saw everyone else, recording work with tapes or notes. Then began the construction of three interlocking plays. She introduced Jess to her husband, a teacher in a prep school who was a frustrated opera singer

15

who didn't want children. We did a lot of improvisations together and the director notated those that worked. Using the house and grounds the director created settings, saying for example of a rockery garden, 'This is a park.' We did individual and joint research, visiting places as well as reading.

We met other characters. One day an Inspector Clouseau type entered wearing sunglasses, who walked into the door because he couldn't see. It was hilarious; we thought, Great, we're to be a three-hander.' But it was an improvisation the director didn't select. He was 'married' to a character with a disability who wanted to run in a marathon for the disabled. There was an improvisation where I met a character from another play, a young pregnant Irish girl. She and I out of mutual need joined forces. She was having a baby and wanted a partner, I wanted a baby. That was the second half of the play which ends as she starts to give birth. It was high comedy, farce almost. At the end of play Jess wore big earrings and was finding herself as young woman without a child.

In Yorkshire the performance was **promenade**. The audience followed the action by moving physically around the rooms and garden. We waited for the audience to arrive. We didn't spend hours getting into character; the work was strong and good at base level. It was very workmanlike and better for it.

Methodology

Later I met Mike Leigh. At the first interview he was very interested in me, not the actress, but my background, and the northern part of me. He asked me to talk about people I knew. He also asked, 'Do you find yourself losing yourself in the parts you play, because they're such strong characters?' I thought he'd want a 'Yes, I get so into my character I lose sight of everything else.' But I don't, so I laughed and said 'No'. He said, 'Brilliant, can you come in on Friday?' Because, of course, you don't lose yourself in parts when you're acting and improvising. You have a strong personal monitor that keeps you aware of the performance aspect and the theatrical side. At the next meeting he asked me to think of people I knew and externalise them physically. Initially I thought of a friend of mine who was having a breakdown. She had a lot of things to latch on to physically and emotionally. He said, 'Don't act,' and had me read a newspaper; there was no dialogue. I sat with the newspaper thinking, '*Don't act*,' so I was really reading the newspaper. Eventually he said, 'Great, you're not acting. But give me something, *externalise* her.' And I thought, '*How?*' My processes were internal. He said, 'Start rocking on the chair and tell me about the effect,' and I realised that's what my friend did. She rocked, often with her legs crossed or doubly crossed – very foetal. I rocked, I read the newspaper and I lost my concentration, so I put the paper down, rocking, getting more grounded, into myself, biting my nails, things like that. It wasn't forced, it became true. When Mike Leigh imposed an external movement on me, that opened floodgates for an internal truth about the character I was portraying.

If I were offering advice to young devisers I would say watch and listen to every kind of character you're interested in. Immerse but keep separate. Study them analytically. Why they dress as they do, why they walk as they do. Look at their body language. Look at the external. Then inhabit. Don the external, but don't expect it to work straight away. Start physicalising, start to use the accent, or not, the shoes you'll use, they all have an impact on the emotional truth of the life of the character. It's no good putting on the costume at the last minute when devising. Even if your character just wears a sloppy jumper, wear it, especially for devising and respond to how it makes you feel.

I use these techniques whenever I work as an actor. After you've learnt the lines for a play, or donned the costumes, there's a way the character sinks deeper into your subconscious. When you say the lines they must come from a real place, they must be truthful even if stylised, or larger than life like **Commedia dell'Arte**. Inhabiting the character physically, externally, in whatever style, will put it on a different level. If the depth of work is there, the audience will believe because you do. There must be truth and that's the difference between great and not great acting. Be as big as you like, but be grounded in truth. That means minute work and research, then you go out with something special.

Summary

Anita is suggesting that stories and situations are created from developing characters with problems to solve. Creating a character and placing them in different situations can create a plot line. Notably Anita uses an external approach drawn from observation to create character – the internal and emotional life then follows.

Questions

- Anita Parry shares a method for devising interlocking plays with an emphasis on truthful characters with problems to solve. How usefully might you draw on this methodology in the creation of your own work?

- Consider the potential of moving into non-typical stage frameworks, e.g. a promenade performance.

- What relationship as actor might you have with the character you are playing?

3 It's Work, not Magic: Devising as a Profession

- artistic directors discussing the nature and significance of devising
- case studies of the devising process
- questions and exercises

This chapter presents the work of four devising companies. Each company is approached from a different angle, and the nature of the questions and tasks is unique to the particular company they follow.

3.1 Trestle Theatre

'There is no mystery, and no dark arts are involved, but if the audience think there are, then there's no harm in that.'
(Toby Wilsher)

Background

Trestle were founded in 1981. Their objective was to bring masks back into popular theatre. They have created 20 shows and toured extensively in the UK and abroad. They have also worked with students and run training courses for businesses. The permanent company now consists of two artistic directors, Toby Wilsher and Joff Chafer, and an administrative team.

In Trestle's shows, the actors hardly speak to each other; rather, meaning is communicated through gesture, physical relationships and the rhythms of the characters. The process of rehearsal is to develop ideas through game playing, improvisation, exercises, research and discussion into a piece of mask and mime work. Trestle's masked characters are individuals with a background, goals and desires. Their uniqueness is that they seem naturalistic though they work *without* spoken language; the characters' gestures and actions emphasise the meaning behind words, the subtext. The masked characters convey individual lives rather than the voice of the people represented through the masked chorus of a Greek tragedy, or the comedy arising from the stock characters of *Commedia dell'Arte* masks.

Trestle Theatre have found a mask form relevant for a contemporary audience.

Toby Wilsher on devising

Toby Wilsher is one of Trestle's two Artistic Directors. Here he shares some views on devising.

Perspectives: a rationale

I went to Middlesex (Poly) with devising my own work in mind; finding other people with the chemistry to be creative together. I didn't want to be an unemployed actor at the whim of other directors and casting personnel. I chose to work with mask because it's about interpretation of gesture, and so non-alienating no matter what the class background of the audience. The work is about how I can stage the observations I make on life around me. I want to tell people and put a theatrical spin on it in doing so. I want to show the audience that devised work is not trashy, hippy or experimental. I want to show audiences that the quality of life can be improved by having a radical theatre experience. It sounds pompous, but I'm always thinking, 'Who am I doing this for?'

Methodology

We'd think of a situation of series of situations – like for *Plastered* a pub, then hospital. We'd talk a lot over the previous tour (12–15 months): 'Let's do the day of a wedding,' 'Let's do the last scene in an unbuilt Spanish hotel.' We'd think of all the things that could happen to characters in those situations. We'd make a big set of masks, about 30, and audition them for characters. We cast about 18. Then we spent about four weeks in the rehearsal room, improvising scenes, putting characters together in a conflict situation, and observing them. We all set up improvisations. We put in props and music. If we weren't on stage, we were out front. In four weeks we had a fun, farcical piece of life.

We wrote a story that took a page of A4. We broke it down into an order of scenes that told the story, maybe 14, 18 or 20 scenes. Each scene was a couple of lines that moved the story on. The kernel of each scene was a visual image, so the whole story could be told visually. We staged the scenes as a moving, visual image like a film. We called that our 'coathanger' – the action that led to the end point of the play. We stuck that on the wall on a big piece of paper, then said, 'Right, we'll start at scene 6.' Then we randomly wrote numbers up to start with, and looked at juxtapositions. We improvised around the visual kernel to put the clothes onto the hanger so each scene was fleshed out from the middle.

That's how we ended with *Top Storey,* which we think is one of the best things we've done. We came up with three versions from the initial coathanger. We used the same structure on the following four or five shows.

The thing I've learnt about devising, the real skill, is letting go of your ideas. Of having ideas and knowing, no matter how important they are to you, that someone else might not think they're that important. You've got to be prepared, the moment you speak an idea, the moment it has left your lips, to know it's no longer yours, because you've planted a seed in someone else's brain, it will take root there and germinate into something else, which is a joy and a frustration. When you devise, you can have as many ideas as you want, but you'll never see the whole lot on stage at the end.

Fool House: an extended case study

'Working with a script is a lot easier, but nowhere near as much fun.' Toby Wilsher

Material for this section has been adapted from Toby Wilsher's account of *The Creation of Fool House* written for *The Advanced Mask Set Notes* and available with the masks. This case study illustrates the mixture of free ideas and rigour that go hand in hand in creating and mounting a full mask production. The process described is a detailed example of a highly structured and well organised rehearsal process. *Fool House* won a Fringe First at the Edinburgh Festival.

- *The company*: collaborative project with Dutch and English actors; Artistic Directors: Joff Chafer and Toby Wilsher; actors: Alan Riley (original founder) and Karina Garnett from England, and Chaya Aschkenasy and Egbert Jan Arnold from Holland
- *Target audience*: people interested in experimental, visual theatre
- *Aims*: to make a play using the slapstick conventions of British **farce** set in an Amsterdam house
- *Genre and style*: a **farce** with masked characters and no spoken text

- *Form and devices*: a two-act play, with an episodic structure. The start and end mirror each other, and are set 200 years earlier. Music to support action. Visual, physical theatre. Act 1 set up predicaments, Act 2 resolved them.

The world of the play

Much of Holland is land reclaimed from the sea. The significance is that the four-storey Amsterdam house in which the action happens stands on the site of a nineteenth-century shipwreck. The play is a *farce*. The action arises through the interaction of the tenants. There are five characters, and three ghosts or 'bog people' played by four actors. The tenants are Dan, an English music conductor, Peter; a secret cross-dresser who has a tortuous relationship with his wife, Lydia; the aged landlady Truus, and Louis, who commits suicide in the first scene. His body hangs on the back of a door in the basement. The play operates on two levels: the interaction of the characters in the rooms, and the antics of the ghosts from the shipwreck.

Fool House: *Daniel, Trundi, Lydia and a bog man. Courtesy of Trestle Theatre.*

The set

Canvas cloth curtain attached to the inside of a carpet roll supported in the lighting rig, curtain down at start so the stage was concealed. The audience needed to recognise the space functioning at different times as different floors in the house. They needed to know whose flat they were in. The stage was end on. Up stage left was a front door frame with knob for entry into flat/s. Inside the door was a step down. The living spaces were at the lower level. Stage left was a sink and cupboard for kitchen, stage right a sofa. On stage right were also two opaque doors, one represented the entrance to the bathroom, and one the entrance to the bedroom. Behind the 'flat' on the higher level, the audience saw a staircase chamber with stairs apparently going up and down. This allowed for farcical business of running up and down stairs. Dan lived at the top, the couple Peter and Lydia below, and Truus on the ground floor. Louis' body hung on the back of a door in the basement.

The opening and subplot

The stage curtain was a calico sailcloth. The show opened with a shipwreck. The cloth was lit from behind creating silhouettes. The sails of a ship danced madly. Characters 'blew' across the stage, as did buckets and other ship items with clearly identifiable shapes. It was accompanied by the sound effects of a storm. The storm quietened, the shipwreck stilled and the canvas was raised like a Roman blind. The house now occupied the space of the shipwreck. There followed a montage of mornings and evenings enabling the audience to grasp the concept of different characters living on different floors. Characters were established, as were the points of their stories. It ended with the suicide of Louis and the arrival of Daniel, the conductor, both played by the same actor. Originally Trestle wanted to employ five actors, but could not afford to pay the fifth. The decision to kill off Louis in the first scene was taken for this reason.

Subsequent scenes showed relationships between characters developing through farcical interfloor coming and going.

There was a subplot in which spirits of sailors, 'bog people', entered the house, through the sofa in the basement. They wanted to free the spirit of the undiscovered suicide. While trying to frighten a burglar by animating the body, they accidentally dropped it out of the window. In trying to reclaim it, they themselves became locked out. Act 2 depicted them trying to get back into the house.

Rehearsal

The rehearsal process fell into three phases: two weeks' studio work, an interim period for reflection and planning, and four weeks' main rehearsal period.

Starting points: that the show would be an English *farce* with much coming and going set in an Amsterdam house; that characters would try to live peacefully with each other but constantly find themselves in different groupings in different flats.

Studio work: in Amsterdam; the rehearsal space was a light, airy chapel with rostra and flats to resemble the set.

Aims: to create a happy and productive team prior to main rehearsal period; to create identities for characters and reasons for being in and out of each others' flats; to explore original ideas.

Warm ups: these are always 'an important part of each rehearsal. They prepare actors for the unexpected physical agility; focus everyone for the task in hand; involve everyone in a shared task; create a sense of ritual leading to taking the art of what you do seriously.' (Toby Wilsher)

Day 1

Objectives: building a team; character discovery; exploring space and movement.

Activities: movement exercises creating an atmosphere of isolation and loneliness in large and confined spaces, for example: working physically to the command of a drum beat; finding and responding to strange objects; moving to different types of music; moving around the space with no noise; getting into character and experimenting with props and objects; working with different *tension states*. Exploration on set of the dynamics of the different floors of the house, for example the *five point exercise*. Trying 'bog people' masks. Starting with entrances; developing to short improvisations.

Outcomes: progress on narrative: Englishman to rent top flat; character commits suicide early on. There would also be an old woman, maybe landlady, and a young couple. The 'bog people' would rise from beneath the house to claim the body.

Challenges: performance styles needed harmonising.

Day 2

Objectives: establishing conventions which show on which floor action takes place; homogenising style; identifying how masks react to different noises and props; directing audience attention to main action on stage.

Activities: freeing, silly games. Experimenting with all characters on stage at once in different flats. Recognised that action is confusing with actors in masks.

Discussion of characters: recognised their need for objectives to make interactions interesting. Why were they in and out of each others flats? 'We also discussed making the couple work dramatically. Peter could be a plumber – really messy, always helping other people but never mending anything in his own flat. She could be a dance teacher and have visiting tap students providing good noise possibilities. What about their relationship? Has he lost interest in her? She could try and spice things up, and decide to fabricate an affair with the Englishman to make her husband jealous. The old woman could be the landlady and cleaner, into spiritualism with friends who visit her for seances.'

Outcomes: character outlines developed, so that now performers could develop them independently.

Day 3

Objectives: to develop the couples' characters.

Activities: improvisations to develop characters with clear objectives, 'We developed strategies to achieve their goals. We turned it into "*one touch football*" so it became clearly action-led. This was so successful we tried another game, with the improvisation working like a tag-wrestling match, people coming in and out, all pursuing their objectives blindly. Lydia tried to get the Englishman into a compromising situation, but all he wanted to do was eat. We found that the more subtle the strategy, the more satisfying it was to watch.' Truus' aim was to keep people in her room. Peter wanted Daniel to be manly. Lydia wanted to make Peter jealous. Dan wanted to be with Lydia because he fancied her.

Research: Historical Museum: clarified identity of bog people as drowned sailors; period clothing and ships' rigging (the set for the storm scenes).

Day 4

Objectives: to foster better improvisation technique; to develop ways the old woman could communicate her feelings through the mask.

Activities: *The Yes Game*; focus improvisations working on action that could be broken into major or minor. This led to the production of the 'clog' scene. Noise was used to throw focus from flat to flat.

Shopping: actors go to flea market for props.

Day 8

Technical manager arrived to discuss set with directors.

Games for fun and enjoyment.

Worked on sequence of choreographed actions and short 'bog people' scenes.

Presented to small audience asking them to focus on clarity of conventions.

 Always present work to a constructive audience during development. They see what you missed.

Actors shopped for costumes on markets

During the interim, directors clarified ideas, determined goals for characters, and worked on the opening. Toby created original music, and Joff and Toby made masks. Set was built by the technical team.

Main rehearsal period

Aims: a structured framework in which the piece is written, rehearsed and polished.

Week 1: Masks and play

Objectives: to discover masks; develop inner lives for characters, and find their speeds and rhythms; create business.

Activities: each performer, using one prop, created three points of 'funny stuff'. Much business emerged, most rejected, some retained, e.g. Lydia on roller skates. The idea of Peter cross-dressing in secret developed. Funny business focused on his predicament, *not* that he was cross-dressing. Rough structure of two acts worked out. Details of narrative and character developed. Directors collated work. Individuals' stories were clarified, broken into a handful of scenes that could be cut up, interspersed through the play, and interwoven with the other stories.

Discussion of style: *farce* was qualified as 'extraordinary things happening to ordinary people'. The farcical elements were pinpointed and explored in the light of this dictum. They decided on a gentler structure in which masks do what they do best – interact.

 It is easy to lose sight of your strengths and follow exciting ideas. This discussion was important in re-establishing direction.

Week 2

Objectives: to develop ideas for scenes and narrative created the previous week.

Activities: many ideas fell by the wayside when subjected to the rigour of structural development. Developed Peter/Lydia relationship: it was plotted through various arguments and stand-offs. An exciting scene developed where, conducting upstairs, Daniel seemed to conduct Lydia and Peter's fight downstairs. Created Daniel's arrival, the revelation of Peter's problem, and opening shipwreck. Once the narrative was clarified, the Company worked hard and effectively at creating performance moments.

Summarised progress: listed scenes to date; characters' stories moved forward. Joff had a key idea which changed the direction of the piece. The bog people would be locked out by Truus while recovering Louis' body, which they had dropped out of the window. Run-through where directors 'shouted scenes and made up missing action as they went along'.

Week 3

Objective: to clarify Act 1.

Activities: three days spent on Act 1 consolidating ideas and setting choreography. Most time spent on detail, ensuring actors communicated what was in their heads to the audience via masks. This required careful plotting. Wednesday – ran Act 1. Started to cut back opening montage from 28 minutes to 10 minutes. Clarified relationships between bog people, other characters and rooms by, for example, exchanging roles. Rough run allowed an overview of the entire piece. Relationships and stories were looked at objectively. Decisions were made about what needed cutting and what needed strengthening.

The main devising period was now over, though new small ideas continued to emerge.

Week 4

Final objectives: make the performance work; get the masks communicating with *each other* and with the *audience* in a clear, economic and truthful manner; make it funnier.

▶ **One of the disciplines of mask rehearsal is the careful and pedantic plotting of movement and gesture to communicate ideas and meaning to an audience. It is only after painstaking choreographing that the scene starts to work and the actors are free to play the mask.**

Activities: 'We started from the beginning and trawled through each scene with a fine tooth comb. A performer was ill on Monday so much of Tuesday was spent recapping. We worked in tedious detail on focus, internal monologue, communication and timing. It is at this stage the directors become really unpopular.'

Be rigorous. The final comb makes the difference between a polished and unpolished performance.

The performers began to work more in costume as they prepared for the really fast changes, particularly the 'bog people', with their full padded costumes, latex feet and hands, and masks and hats. Despite taking three weeks to make, the hands were finally cut as they did not work on stage – a painful decision taken in the interests of the piece.

Worked out ending and finished the week with a run of Act 2.

Week 5: final week

Objective: to prepare for performance.

Activities: each *Act* was given 90 minutes hard labour, the focus being on the performance of the mask. Then a costume run and first notes. The last two days were spent in dress rehearsals. The directors gave notes and final adjustments were made.

Production week and opening

Set, costumes and props moved into Bowen West Theatre, Bedford. Light and sound were plotted. There was a *ten-hour technical rehearsal*, and then three dress rehearsals during which small invited audiences gave valuable feedback to directors. The first preview (pre-opening-night performance) was nervous and slightly rushed. The timing of scenes, the actions and reactions, were based entirely on the characters' internal monologues, so after the preview they had a rehearsal that should have been earlier, a run-through without masks where the performers articulated everything they were thinking. To get the mask's timing right, the actor must be clearly focused on the character's *thoughts*, and must not lapse into conversation. This helped some scenes that were not quite right. As the play commenced on tour, it developed, tightened and assumed a life of its own.

Summary

Toby and his company have a very focused rehearsal process where objectives are continually set and techniques to achieve them employed. They work with essential props and costume as early as possible.

Questions

- To what extent do you feel you should be focused on your time and objectives in rehearsal?

- How might your devising group use music and sound, action-based rehearsal techniques and exercises, and props and costume to move a piece forward? What might the technical implications be for resources and the technical rehearsal?

- Consider how mime, mask, and puppetry might enrich your own work.

3.2 Improbable Theatre

'A will to enlarge the language of theatre that is thrilling to behold and essential to absorb.' (Michael Coveney)
'People who say yes get rewarded with adventures. People who say no get rewarded with security. Too much security is boring and too much not knowing is scary. The audience don't want to watch everyone looking terrified on stage.'
'Be nice to each other. Just be nice.' (Lee Simpson)

Background

Improbable Theatre has an international reputation for its innovative and extraordinary shows. Set and props are found or made from cheap materials, and through the imagination of performers and audience are transformed into objects of significance. Improbable was founded in 1996 by Phelim McDermott, Lee Simpson and Julian Crouch. Tired of working in buildings where necessary bureaucracy stifled spontaneity and creativity, they chose to return to the essence of what makes theatre vital, immediate and accessible – a live contract between performer and performer, and audience and performer. *Improbable*'s approach to performance is unusual and frightening for performers. They deliberately build uncertainties into shows by leaving gaps which aren't scripted or set and often *stop* actors learning lines. They *improvise in front of the audience*. The result is an electric energy between audience and performers; and performances that evolve each night on stage.

Actors, audience and spontaneity

Phelim McDermott and Lee Simpson are two of *Improbable Theatre's* Artistic Directors. Here they share approaches to devising. In discussion they refer to *Shockheaded Peter,* a dark piece of music theatre which subverts the conventions of music theatre. It was adapted from Heinrich Hoffmann's *Struwwelpeter,* written in 1844. The stories are grotesquely funny, cautionary tales for children. *Cinderella* was a stage play based on Angela Carter's *Ashputtel.* Both were performed at The Lyric Theatre, Hammersmith.

Perspectives on devising: a rationale for spontaneous improvisation

'If you set out to create a good play, you'll fail. If you set out to get excited about being on stage and the words which might come out when you don't know what to say, you'll more likely end up able to devise and create your own work. On stage the need for change in pace, narrative and structure become obvious. The audience know, and if you can be excited, not fearful, you can hear what the audience wants.'

Methodology

'In rehearsal you spend the weeks creating the rules of the world the characters inhabit; the environment, or how the characters behave in that world. *Shockheaded Peter* had a strong structure with massive gaps. The characters inhabited a backstage world in rehearsal created through improvising. The set was visualised from this.' It was illusory and fantastical, the interior of a Victorian house in which anything could happen, peopled by strange archetypes of Victorian society, and a roving band of musicians. Architectural lines, created by a series of doors stage right and left, converged to a vanishing point. The world was distorted and sinister, like the piece itself. 'If you've explored that world enough and remember it's going to be in front of an audience, you can do whatever you want in front of an audience.' *Improbable's* rehearsal process is committed to six principles:

- Spontaneous improvisation always as if in front of an audience
- Working integrally with the design and technical team
- Doing before talking
- Saying 'Yes' to ideas. 'If someone says, 'Have you got the car keys?' don't say 'No'. Say, 'Yes, they're here, and I fixed the engine." It

means a scene will happen. They're rules to create stories, but they're also a set of attitudes to life.'
* Looking for inspiration in mistakes
* Building in uncertainties to maintain surprise in performance 'It's magical. It's the only advantage theatre has over movies and TV. The impulse to sort it and plan before kills it before it has a chance to prove itself.'

Trusting your creativity

'Working spontaneously means trusting yourself as a performer, trusting in your own creativity and having the constant desire to surprise yourself and the audience. You can do all sorts of things in five weeks rehearsal, but at the end of the day, something else happens on stage and ideally it's something you didn't plan; its transformative; it surprises you. Some ideas are cherished, you want them included, but the rehearsal process doesn't lead you there. You can't know the end of your journey before you begin. And the joke, 'Wouldn't it be good if everyone did this with buckets on their heads', is the seed of creating a really interesting show.'

The community of theatre

Trust and support among performers, in rehearsal and on stage, are crucial in nurturing creativity and performance skills. To create honest work company members have to look after each other. 'Be nice to each other. Just be nice. Be there together. If someone bails out saying, for example, "The show may be rubbish but I'm going to be OK" or "learn my lines," sack them! More trouble comes when someone in the group is absolutely terrified and they pretend everything is alright; it saps the energy out of the process and it's not honest. If someone says, "I'm really terrified" and bursts into tears, and others say "So am I, it's scary," you can move on. The audience like to see a group of people working together and looking after each other in difficult circumstances.' Performers in *Shockheaded Peter* weren't allowed to learn their lines. 'On the second night in Leeds, Martyn kept singing the wrong words to the wrong tune. Eventually he said, "This isn't working. I think I'd better go," and walked off stage. There was nothing on stage, Then Julian Bleach [an actor in the show] leapt on and did a speech from Richard III. It was one of the funniest things I've [Phelim] ever seen, and it was created out of chaos. Julian made sure Martyn didn't look stupid. That for me is a political statement – about theatre as a way of showing how people can work together as a community and look after each other. We try and do that. That's why people are interested. Keith Johnstone said, "If there are four of you on stage – your job is to make the other three look fantastic. That means at any point there are three people trying to make you look fantastic."'

Total Theatre and puppets

Working integrally with the design and technical team are important. Julian Crouch as director/designer is present throughout the rehearsal period. Another unique element in *Improbable*'s work is the animation of newspaper or other 'found' objects into puppets. In *Improbable*'s version of *Cinderella*, newspaper was transformed into a variety of animate objects including a cat, and a horse on which Cinderella and the Prince rode to the mountains. The process of transformation was magical. The principle of creation is not origami; the directors stopped performers 'making cats'. Rather, results came from moving objects in a way that was a game everyone played, working together in a certain rhythm, and believing in the creation.

70 Hill Lane

'A trickster spirit with a devilish wit, solid objects that pass through walls, and a house with an untold secret. Part autobiography, part fantasy and dream, this show creates a haunting world of childhood yearning through an extraordinary synthesis of storytelling, improvisation, object animation, live music and ... sellotape.'

This case study illustrates a process based approach to making a show. The Company chose not to create a fixed piece of theatre, but a show which would shift in content from performance to performance. Preparation was to discover and develop the rules of the world through the creation of material, or '*stories*'. They chose to risk because they had faith in their ability to create and perform. They worked spontaneously, creatively and with trust. They sought surprise, excitement and truth. *70 Hill Lane* won awards in New York, London, Manchester and Egypt.

The company

Made by Phelim McDermott, Julian Crouch, Lee Simpson and Guy Dartnell; Steve Tiplady (animation); Ben Park (music); Colin Grenfell (lighting).

The world of the play

70 Hill Lane, the house which the author/performer grew up in, is the central image explored through re-creation of the past at Hill Lane, in dreams and in the present in Phelim's Brixton flat.

The set

The audience needed to recognise when they were in 70 Hill Lane, Phelim's flat, or a dream. It also needed to be portable for touring. 12 rostra made an acting space of 4880 x 3660 mm (16x12 ft). Each rostrum had four holes to take metal poles that slotted in and out during performance. The set was constructed from poles, newspaper and sellotape during performance.

Genre and style

The show defies any obvious labels. A synthesis of stand-up comedy and theatrical storytelling may be a starting point.

70 Hill Lane. As Phelim told the story he stuck small objects onto the sellotape.

Form and devices

A synthesis of theatrical storytelling, puppetry, improvisation and song and live music to create a funny, magical, haunting world in which the inanimate became animate. Main story told by Phelim using direct address and demonstration, alongside mime to indicate doorways etc. Steve and Guy were often on stage playing other characters, making house structures from sellotape and making and manipulating puppets. All had street clothes on. Ben improvised with a range of instruments, usually to create and enhance mood and atmosphere. Lee, and sometimes Julian, acted as an outside eye setting up environments in which the performers could improvise, and shaping improvisations where necessary.

Summary of the play

The show started with the creation of a human figure, then a fairy story. Three interrelated narratives, one present tense, one past, and one dreamlike were fractured, interwoven and told episodically. Phelim was the main storyteller, with Guy and Steve helping. The Company manipulated mood and atmosphere, making quick transitions from funny scenes to ghostly scenes and vice versa. This came partly from placement of stories, also music, tone of voice, sound, silence, and at times the ripping sound of sellotape unrolling. The play ended with another fairy story/poem, then the creation of a puppet drawing the symbols and metaphors of the spirit and ordinary world together.

Description of performance action

This description shows how elements of theatre combined in engaging and taking the audience willingly, imaginatively and with belief into the world of *70 Hill Lane*. Its focus is *structure*. Narratives were fractured, stories were always surprising, yet the piece moved to a climax. Varying pace, mood and atmosphere kept the audience engaged. Direct address made the show very intimate; street clothes made the actors vulnerable and exposed. They were themselves. There was no costume or make-up to hide behind. Use of simple set, varied lighting, minimal props, and live improvised music drew the audience into the world of *70 Hill Lane*. The elements combined to create a complex theatre piece which worked on a number of levels.

- Black stage: light came up on Phelim at table centre stage looking at a newspaper. He picked up the newspaper, moving it to create a puppet.

He was joined by Guy and Steve, who built more of the puppet – a human figure. A flute played single notes wistfully. They walked the puppet down the table and spun it slowly into the air until they held it centre stage high in the air, transformed into a circle lit with a hand-held light. It had become the moon. Phelim walked to front centre stage and sat cross-legged in a small white light. He told the audience a fairy story of how the moon witnessed the birth of an oxygen-starved 'cinder-black baby', and of how that baby's mother 'roared the life' back to her child.

- Front stage lit, Phelim introduced himself, Steve and Guy to the audience. He explained that the show would be about his encounter with a poltergeist when he was a boy.
- Set for Brixton flat brought on; two double chairs indicated furniture. Story about 'living in Brixton'. Steve played Phelim, Phelim played his alter ego, the critic: 'You're always losing things …'
- Chairs off. Hill Lane setting built. Four metal poles placed in corners of stage, connected by sellotape. Story about Hill Lane. Phelim aged 14/15 described the house: 'Shall I show you round?' Guy and Steve created sellotape tables, windows and staircases as needed. As Phelim described and demonstrated the playroom on the attic floor, unsettling music played. 'I don't like to look in there, I don't like to think what's in there.'

This was the introduction to the story of the poltergeist. The poltergeist narrative started and stopped throughout the piece, interrupted by other stories, some from the present, some not. After three other stories about Phelim's family, the poltergeist story was taken up again.

- 'Whoever it is, has got into my house.' Sellotape was noisily taped between poles at eye height. As Phelim demonstrated the story he stuck little objects – a clothes peg, a toy car, nail scissors, a plastic spoon – onto the sellotape. Under stage lights they looked as if they floated on a laser beam. As he told of the poltergeist throwing things down the stairs, objects fell randomly from the tape.
- Interrupted by lighting change, flat furniture was brought in and three stories about 'living in Brixton' were told. The sequence ended as Steve and Guy built a 'bed' structure from steel poles and wooden board. Phelim lay down under a small light. He said, 'Sometimes I hope something will happen when I fall asleep.' As he talked Guy and Steve pulled a Copydex layer of glue off the table top and wrapped him up. It was ragged and smothering. It made him like a ghost.

Breathless music accompanied. Another newspaper puppet, taller, emerged from behind Phelim and walked off toward the light. Lights came up and he struggled out of the skin.

- The prologue 'fairy story' was retold as an event – Phelim's 'mother' told him how he'd been born black and still, and that, 'I shook you, I shook you, I shook you, and you came back to life.'
- A dream story in which Phelim re-encountered the house and poltergeist in the present. Disturbing background music, fight and embrace of the poltergeist – Phelim darting and rushing round space, footlights contorted his face with strange shadows.
- Phelim sat on the table and continued the poltergeist story. Guy and Steve made a sellotape door hole in the 'attic'.
- Story about returning to the house as a grown up.
- Poltergeist story continued: Phelim crouched in his 'bed' staring terrified at attic stairway. Lighting on sellotape made it unearthly, self-generating light sources. It was the most terrifying night of his life. He wanted to escape from his room but the lights shone on the attic steps. He fought through the corridor of lights to the safety of his parents' room.
- A story about the flat.
- A story about the house now. An old man played by Guy emerged. Roaring music accompanied a fight between Phelim and the man as poltergeist.
- Fairy story/poem told by Phelim squatting and looking as though through the attic door. Footlights created up-shadows on his face making it strange, and he distorted his features and voice – it was about him and the poltergeist being one: 'Polty says … your troublemaker is your teacher …'
- Final image: discordant loud music, lots of sellotape screetchily stretched round four poles, then ripped down and rolled and pulled into a luminous puppet, three feet high, with large head and scrunched ball feet. The saxophone played hauntingly. The three actors walked it slowly across the stage. The lights made it golden and silver. It was ethereal and beautiful. They moulded it into a round ball – the moon. Phelim held it up centre stage. The light overhead faded and there was darkness. End.

70 Hill Lane. 'Polty' sellotape ghost puppet. Sketch by Julian Crouch.

The process of creation – rehearsing *70 Hill Lane*

Starting points: that the show would be about Phelim's house and his encounter with a poltergeist. Phelim's knowledge of the architecture and contents of his house. The decision that lots of newspaper and a little sellotape would be materials for settings – perhaps the house built of newspaper stuck onto sellotape. The desire to make the audience laugh.

The Company rehearsed in a church in the East End of London with lots of junk. They brought newspaper and sellotape. They had four weeks.

Aims: to tell a story the audience were interested in, entertain them, and make them laugh; to make a performance that merged stand up comedy with theatre; to create something personal that became something universal.

Activities: the company spent three and a half weeks experimenting. Lee and sometimes Julian were outside eyes. The rehearsal period generated much material. Phelim told stories each day. Without set or props, he presented the architecture of the house: 'I'll show you what the house is like. Over here is a table, a box my Gran kept her knick-knacks in. There's a dog down there.' Different places and objects prompted different stories, for example a photograph of his mother, or a glass case with dolls his dad brought back from business trips. Sometimes the stories were funny, then there was consideration of how to present these to an audience. Often that which made them laugh, or felt too outrageous for the show, was what they eventually chose to include.

Guy and Steve joined in playing necessary roles. 'Guy might play my mum and I'd tell him what to say, or I might play my mum and he'd play me, so we'd swap different roles round.' The company created an environment for Phelim, his flat, and put him in it. His work was to visualise it. Lee might say, 'Just be in your flat for a bit and wait for something interesting.' Phelim told stories, some about being in the flat after going drinking. This generated a lot of material. It created a security in *Improbable*'s ability to develop that world on stage. For recalling scenes in the flat, they sometimes used a video camera and wrote down the actor's words.

During the second week, Julian presented the idea of sticking steel poles into a pin board of rostra blocks. Sellotape could be stretched to create different structures. In one rehearsal they built the whole ground floor from tape and newspaper, keeping the focus on what looked interesting, stretching and playing with it like puppetry. The sellotape was more interesting than the newspaper. The lighting designer, Colin, came to a rehearsal with hand-held lights, which on sellotape looked almost like laser beams. 'It looked really fantastic in the space.' They planned to make the ghost of animated sellotape.

Accidental discoveries were vital to the process. For example, Steve thought they could use dried Copydex glue to 'peel the ghost off the floor'. 'We tried but it looked terrible. Later we covered the tabletop in glue. I told and we acted a dream story. Colin had lights. I lay on the table; they peeled and wrapped me in glue. It was fantastic. We never did it again but we knew it would be in the show.'

They generated lots of pieces of A4 paper with headings, *e.g.* '*The Day the Poltergeist Arrived*'. Phelim wrote two fairy tales, *The Cinder Baby and The Moon* and *Polty*. They chose not to put these in order until the middle of the last week of rehearsal, then they selected a potential structure. They knew some images would definitely be included.

Technical rehearsal

Improbable chose to take three days for the technical rehearsal. They walked and talked through the show on stage. Time was short and decisions were made quickly. The lighting designer created lighting states around them. They chose to open with the making of the puppet, then the fairy story. These framing devices gave the action a mythical quality. Anything which didn't work in the proposed structure was swapped or cut. Technical problems of how to get from A to B were addressed. Within a loose structure determined by technical demands, there were spaces for improvisation.

Summary

Improbable Theatre's methodology blurs the distinction between process and product. The company ensure they have freedom to work spontaneously in performance, guaranteeing freshness and excitement for themselves and the audience.

Questions

- How many 'stories' are contained in *70 Hill Lane*? Do you think *Improbable* told the same stories every performance? Or do you think they created new ones each night? Which would be more exciting?

- What do you find inspirational in their philosophy and work? What have been your most exciting performance moments?

- How might you use spontaneous improvisation in rehearsal and performance?

- How does the Company use props in their work? Might this influence you?

- Try playing with props – decide on an object, e.g. baskets, play 'that looks like …' Experiment with newspaper, be interested in it, and be honest about whether it is communicating anything to an audience or not.

A 45-minute practical workshop

Aims: Spontaneous play-making with stories and props. Saying yes. Making everyone on stage look good.

Method:

1. Warm-up with *The Yes Game*.
2. Work in groups of 3–6. One person will work as the story teller. Everyone suggests a title for the story, maybe a story you all know like *Cinderella*, or something new like 'The Ghost House', or 'My Holiday in Spain'. The storyteller chooses which to work with. The storyteller starts as the 'I'. Everyone else improvises to support the storyteller and the development of the story through providing props, playing characters, being furniture, plugging gaps, etc. Find as many ways of endorsing the story as possible.
3. Work with the objects you find in the space to transform them into something else.
4. Towards the end of your session, summarise each improvisation or 'story' and write it on a separate piece of paper. Spend five minutes selecting and juxtaposing the stories for performance. Perform your work without stopping.

3.3 The Northern Stage Ensemble

'Audiences have big imaginations, brains, feelings, eyes and ears. We want to create great theatre, and build lasting, meaningful relationships.' Alan Lyddiard

Background

Alan Lyddiard is the artistic director of Newcastle Playhouse. He oversees the creative output of an important repertory theatre. He is also Artistic Director of *The Northern Stage Ensemble*, and under his direction the Company has gained a regional, national and international reputation for its exciting style of physical and visual theatre and its commitment to participatory projects. He is a visionary with a concern for the relationships between audience and performer, and performer and community. His pieces are of energy and life, honesty and truth. It is this truth he seeks in all his work.

Alan Lyddiard's approach

Rationale

The two motivating forces in this company are to make great theatre, and make relationships with people. To achieve that we do a range of different things connected with creating a project around something that's inspired us. *Clockwork Orange* and *Animal Farm* are two texts that inspired us. We wanted to use these as the catalyst for a range of projects that would include a performance at their centre.

Our background is in the community. Theatre in Education, Community Theatre and the Arts Centre movement informs a lot of the work we do. I saw a piece directed by Alain Platel involving professional actors playing an equal role with young people. They'd made an incredibly arty piece of work with dodgems at a circus. It was fantastic and dangerous and brilliant and beautiful and I would aspire to work like that in the future, where I could have young people and professional actors creating work together. The people on our stage should be like the people on the street. The people watching have got to see themselves in the work we do in some way. This is theatre that's making relationships with people.

'I'm studying the idea that textual language is a substitute for meaning. I'm interested in exploring what Jacques Lacan (French psychoanalyst, 1901–81) calls 'the symbolic state'. I'm trying to find the reality of that, and find a way of dealing with meaning that doesn't use text. The real state is beyond language but can be expressed in poetry and visual images – that's what we're searching for. The text of *Animal Farm* is 26 pages long, the show is 90 minutes. Most of the piece is visual images with sound. I'm trying to invent a language that expresses my needs in theatre: I say *'performer'* not 'actor', *'spectator'* not 'audience'; I create *'environment'* not 'sets', because I want to try to articulate what I'm thinking.

The company

Following a major award from the National Lottery, *Northern Stage Ensemble* established a pilot Ensemble Company comprising a permanent team of performers and other staff who will work together on a continuous basis for three years to create theatre and encourage participation in the arts.

The choosing of people is very important. I don't want actors. I want people that are vibrant, exciting, beautiful, energetic, scary and answer me back and give me a hard time. And I want them to express themselves completely on stage. What I want to see is the performer and the performance at the same time. We always have people who reflect the energy or feeling of place; we don't have actors from drama schools on the whole. We have some young performers we've trained over a period of time from different sorts of colleges, some with GNVQs, others with degrees in Performing Arts. Each trainee has an individual training programme, which includes writing a log of what they learnt or are considering.

We have Company class every morning from 9.30 to 11.00 which includes meditation, T'ai Chi, and 'Opening the Natural Voice'. It is a key element in establishing trust and respect in the Company. I work a lot on sense of self, or being, rather than acting or pretending. For me, it's the basic premise on which my work starts. Specialists on voice and movement and trainers from other areas also work with the Company. Companies from all over the world come to perform in our theatre. When they come they work with our actors during the day, and also with the greater community we are part of. Those things make the kind of performance quality we are looking for.

Methodology

The Ensemble is a way of life. We reinvent ourselves and emerge in different ways, like magpies picking things up and putting them in one place. We are cross art, physical, poor, rough, **Grotowski**, meditation, a bit of this and that. I recognise every day what I can learn from the people I'm working with. The work we do with special needs, with young offenders, it's not add-on, it's crucial. In terms of content, there's no point doing easy stuff. Theatre can do anything: murder; rape; kill; be killed; anything. It is a safe place for these issues to be assessed, talked about, debated. On the *Clockwork Orange* tour at Llandudno, there was a demonstration outside the theatre: 'Keep rape off the stage'. My question is, 'Where would you like it?' All the most beautiful things can be explored, and all the most difficult, hardest things can be explored. You can do that and feel OK. It may be disturbing and difficult, but where else can you do it?

You need to articulate very carefully and clearly to performers what is required and how they can achieve it. That is the most difficult thing to do because they all come with baggage: their past history; their experiences of theatre and life. To put 13 people in a room and make them a cohesive ensemble is complicated and difficult. We have arguments about the way things have to be done: how we can get closer to what I require of 'you' the performer, and how I can get closer to what 'you' the performer feel about it. That has to be a big part of the process.

Honesty in performance is very important. I'm trying to put in front of you a human being exposing themselves vulnerably. That is the most powerful thing we've got together, people able to say, 'This is me and I want to express who I am and to communicate that to you.' That is the most powerful, exciting thing about living. That's what I'm trying to do on the stage. In the meantime I'm giving lots of very interesting visual images, and keeping you inspired by some of the thoughts and images around the piece. The bottom line is you're seeing a living human on the stage. Put someone on stage, shine a light on them so you can see them. That is beautiful.

I think people are put off by seeing how clever others are. Audiences want to see how frightened people are. At *Northern Stage* we're more interested in vulnerability. We enjoy stimulating debate. We want that as equals. Theatre says we're very clever, beautiful, nice and smart and we speak beautifully, and you should be enjoying yourself. That's crass. **Peter Brook** talks about Rough Theatre and Ritual Theatre and *Empty Space*. He speaks very simply about theatre. He says it better than anyone.

Animal Farm

'We don't make plays, we make projects.' Alan Lyddiard

Alan Lyddiard describes the preparation for *Animal Farm*. In doing so he shows how structure, style and content made meaning for a contemporary society. *Northern Stage's Animal Farm* has been in a process of evolution since the first Studio production in 1993. The current production was rehearsed for six weeks in a church hall. It was funded by a Lottery Grant.

The Company

Directed by Alan Lyddiard, designed by Neil Murray, choreography by Frank McConnell, with eight of the company's performance ensemble;

The world of the play

Animal Farm is a novel written by George Orwell in 1944, depicting the dangers of communism. The play takes the farm setting from the novel. The action, set in a farmyard, started with the arrival of a group of refugees dressed in clothes recognisable from TV as Kosovan. They set down their bags and packs, and enacted their version of *Animal Farm*, a struggle for power. Dressed in vest and pants with hobnailed boots on feet and hands they became horses, pigs and other animals. The play shows the animals' struggle for better conditions, leading to the overthrow and eviction of the farmer; a new regime led by the pigs; and the casting out of animals who preferred the old system. Eventually the pigs become 'human'. The circle has turned right round. In the meantime, a few animals have been killed, and more been made homeless. It is also the story of conflict over land and culture, dispossession and the search for a new life.

The set

The play was performed on an open stage. Flats on three sides were made from corrugated iron with doorways for exits and entrances. The floor was covered with a thick layer of 'mud' (compost). There was a bath full of water stage right, and a wooden step ladder upstage. During the show this was used by Squeaker to enable the hanging and re-hanging of the Animal Manifesto chalked up on wooden boards (the final one read '*All animals are equal, but some animals are more equal than others*'). There were a large number of wooden pallets which the performers built into structures during the performance.

Alan Lyddiard tells how the design evolved: 'I have a long standing working relationship between Frank McConnell, choreographer and our designer Neil Murray. I want people to understand what I feel. On principle, we don't make decisions about how a piece should look. I'll say, 'Mud', Neil says, 'Palace', Frank says, 'It's a nightmare, what are we going to do?' Then he'll painstakingly mark out a way of drawing it up and making it happen. Neil will get thousands of photographs as visual aids and cover the whole of his room. A photo depicting people with boots on hands and feet inspired the idea for doing the same with the animals; the hob nailed boots on hands and feet kept the metaphor of animals as working people of the land very much in mind.'

Genre and style

Physical theatre.

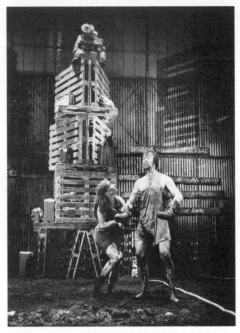

Animal Farm: building the windmill from pallets.

Form and devices

Fractured performance style with fast, choreographed movement to *Test Department* techno music depicted animals working very hard. The images were often broken by sudden moments of stillness or changes in pace or direction. The narrative was developed in the spaces between the choreographed action. The actors took on the quality of their animals while staying recognisably human. The action moved from apparent disorder to order. Lighting often worked in time with the music and the physical action. It was designed to create shadow and light, and pick out small areas of the stage in which action happened. Costumes were minimal and unglamorous, making the actors appear vulnerable and naked.

Description of opening sequence

The play opened with the arrival of a straggling line of refugees bearing heavy loads. They entered the barn-like space, looked around as if they had come to a safe place, and set down their bags. They talked naturally to each other. They undressed to white pants and vests. These soon became muddy and discoloured after exposure to mud and water. Loud beat music played and they started work – assuming animal physicalisation they ran, lifted pallets, threw pallets, built and unbuilt structures. This was the work of the farm animals. They climbed in the bath to cool down, or dipped their heads under water, and shook them to produce a stream of water under the lights.

The Process of creation

'Our starting point for the first production was fighting in Bosnia and refugees travelling all over the Balkans. Now things are no better. In Kosovo and East Timor, there are literally thousands of refugees travelling across the country into some place not their home, trying to find a new world for themselves. This is their Utopian vision. Our version of the play is about repression of a people and nationhood. We set it in a world which recognises the Eastern European atmosphere. We use Macedonian music, also refugee clothing you'd recognise from TV.

I went to Kosovo and Macedonia because it was important to understand more about the refugee feelings they would have. I felt inadequate. I saw babies left by their mothers begging in the street; men crying in corners; aid workers being like John Wayne; journalists wired and completely drunk because they could not cope with what they'd seen. Just to sit in the middle for a moment was important for me to make sense of what I was doing on the stage. It was about trying to understand what's going on in the world, and communicating some of this through theatre.

In terms of adapting the text, it's Orwell's words, then a bit of Wooldridge who first worked it with TAG TiE Company, and bits of all the actors who've ever played it. The actual script is 26 pages. The performance lasts for 90 minutes. Most of the time is spent on physical work which we devised together in rehearsal.

This piece started with a four-week rehearsal period in January 1993. We are still rehearsing in October 1999. Each time the show is toured, it is remade. The first three weeks were spent on physical work, in the fourth week we worked with text and put it in order. There was then a four-day technical rehearsal. Time was the discipline. We had to reach deadlines while keeping as open, chaotic and difficult as possible in order that new things could arise. I kept the decision making process as late as possible.

Creating material is very important. Throughout the rehearsal period I'm looking for material, every day I'm compiling material. A lot is rubbish, but sometimes it's fantastic and will come back in performance. There are specific choices, for instance the story of a man with a carrier bag which he punches holes into, so he can have a shower. It's seen just for a moment but it's a complex image which is strengthened by accompanying music. I don't plan, and want a lot of conclusions quickly. My personal target is to get a conclusion from each day.

The biggest challenge is to be believable. A Spanish director we work with slaps people and says, 'You're lying.' Acting is pretending. To express something fundamental to a group of people in front of you, you have to enter into that challenge of talking as a human being, and showing what human beings suffer and what they aspire to, and show their resilience. That's going to be very difficult, so I say to performers, 'You have to work very hard to learn physical skills; and be brave enough to climb high rickety structures; and throw yourselves about a lot, and you must not pretend for one minute that you are an animal, or a character in a play. You must be yourself fighting for a character, fighting to understand Boxer, Clover, Napoleon.' The most difficult thing for actors is not to act. Every actor in the world is trained to act, I train them not to act. They feel they are letting the side down if they're not showing me everything they do, endlessly; 'I'm being a very clever pig.'

In rehearsal I talked a bit about my experiences. Then I got them to walk up and down the road with heavy luggage and sweat a lot. I made them work hard, and was a vicious fascist going 'faster, faster, faster'. Then I said, 'This is what it's like.' I run around and make them run around. This show is about physical work. They don't act, they do a lot of tasks. They move windmills, they rush through the mud, and they have lots of orders. I say, 'You do that and you do that'; 'You have to do that completely, don't pretend, don't act, do it.' Once they've got it I give them a bit more, so they're always striving. Physically, the piece is about their physical will to be resilient to what I throw at them. It's like an obstacle race, and they have to run through it as fast, as well, as completely as they can and they have to enjoy every minute, like the army. The reality is every time you see them on stage, the physical work is real. They're really tired. They go into training to lift big heavy pallets. I can't lift them. They are very small people picking up enormous pallets. It's that that makes sense of being a refugee. This is what makes sense of the meaning beyond words. Physically struggling to do something actually difficult which makes you tired, resentful and angry at times, and also determined, is the essence of what the piece is about. My piece based on *Animal Farm* says, 'There is hope, there is a future, and whatever happens to you, you can keep going, to the next refugee camp, the next muddy field, as long as there is still somewhere to go. If you're alive, you can keep going.' Orwell says, 'Power corrupts – that's human nature' – I'm saying, 'Human nature is bigger than this.' In doing the work, they show that and it becomes meaningful for the audience.

The technical rehearsal is a good, long, and very important time. I love it. I'm very much about framing things. I create worlds and pictures, inhabited I hope by very interesting people. They have wonderful things to say to each other. The process of making that as finished as possible is the most important time. It's like a film maker doing the editing. The decisions are 'I'll have that shot, and that shot, and it will be quick. It will go zoom', 'a bit of music', 'linger on that hand'. It is a very charged atmosphere, electric – you're up against time and the show's about to happen.

Summary

Alan's philosophy for his ensemble is very focused. He sees the performers' task as showing the vulnerability of being human, through ensuring truth and endeavour in performance. He is concerned that the audience recognise themselves in the performers, and deliberately chooses not to work with trained actors. His performances draw on multi-media technology, and there is always an edge of danger.

Questions

- How might Alan's approach to performers and performance change people's attitudes to watching and participating in theatre?
- What do you think the role of theatre should be in the 21st century?
- How is the audience response controlled through the visual/design image?
- How might you build an ensemble?

3.4 Passe-Partout

> 'Never doubt that a group of thoughtful, committed citizens can change the world. Indeed it is the only thing that ever has.'
> (Margaret Mead)

Introduction

Passe-Partout is a UK-based company founded in 1986 by educationalists working to develop the individual's responsibility to society. They operate on a national and international level. Projects in Britain have included programmes for tackling racism and bullying. International projects include, in Ghana, teaching the importance of safe driving and, in Kenya, educating parents in the need to send their daughters to school by exploring the social cost of not doing so. They are committed to community partnerships on issue-based learning. They work with a range of schools, universities, teachers and community centres. They have developed twenty pieces of theatre, most of which have toured in Britain and abroad. They have evolved a methodology which ensures that the views and experiences of the host community are reflected in the contents of the piece. They aim to provoke thought, involvement and a desire to make changes.

Methodology

Passe-Partout works through a combination of questionnaires, interviews and theatre. One step is to identify a set of key questions around the issue under analysis and some possible answers. Another is to determine community members' responses to the questions. These activities can be interwoven with performance, for example by asking the questions, or handing out questions, before or during performance, or maybe as a separate phase, with the theatre piece built on the outcomes of questionnaires. Both the questions and the answers come from the community *Passe-Partout* is working with.

The process starts with the community. In a project on bullying, for example, drama students made a questionnaire which sought to collect views, attitudes, and incidences. The students collected responses from across the school community. When they started to make their theatre piece, all views of the community were reflected in the piece. As they had been consulted, the community had a vested interest in the piece.

Because their views were represented at a distance, the process broadened their understanding of the issues at stake.

The *Passe-Partout* process reflects the particular community, with its particular set of social circumstances. The work is fundamentally about asking questions, analysing the responses and portraying these as theatre to provoke thought and engage dialogue. Performers are gatherers of information as well as presenters of synthesis. They learn the most from the project. When Passe-Partout sets up a project abroad, part of the remit is to train the performing group in the work, and leave them to develop it through performing themselves, and developing other performance groups. There is a multiplier effect, so the approach gets disseminated. *Passe-Partout* also run training courses for European teachers and community workers interested in developing skills in devising social documentary theatre.

Breaking the Chains – The Story of Land

This case study illustrates

- theatre as an authoritative account of peoples lives;
- theatre to promote self responsibility;
- the use of information to authenticate performance;
- adaptation for a different audience;
- the role drama can play in addressing and challenging development issues.

The context

Bangladesh is an Islamic country. There are strict cultural codes relating to the roles of men and women:

- each village has a chairman who has certain responsibilities and privileges;
- the villages in which the work was carried out have organised their own committees of men's group and women's groups. Their role is to ensure participation and protection;
- Most of the village people are poor and almost none are literate.

Breaking the Chains was created and toured in Bangladesh, France and the UK.

The company

This was a collaborative project with performers and community workers from three local organisations working at grass roots level to create an interactive theatre piece which gave a voice to the poorest in Bangladesh. This team worked for four weeks with Michèle Young, Passe-Partout's Artistic Director. There were 12 performers, the number of seats in the minibus. Selection was on the basis of different attributes and experience. For instance, an elderly gentleman gave credibility in the eyes of the village people; there was a translator, there was a musician, and there was someone who knew the ways of the village people. Michèle Young directed the play.

The world of the play

The play is set in the villages near Dinajpur in Bangladesh. Its subject is the injustice suffered by the poor at the hands of the rich and powerful. It demonstrates injustices, and shows how communities have countered it through community action in, for example, the setting up of groups to buy collectively controlled land.

Target audience and aims

The broad aims were to promote changes in the power structure. There were three versions of the piece for three target audiences.

1) *The Story of Land – Village People,* ninety minutes, Dinajpur district. The *aims* for the village audience were to involve them in an education programme which would affect them directly, to empower by clarifying injustices and opening discussion to remedy them.
2) *The Story of Land,* with dialects adapted and more statistical information, had for target audience NGOs and officials in Dhaka, the regional capital (ninety minutes). Aims for the Dhaka audience, the middle classes with power and influence, were to increase awareness of injustices in the system and thus encourage them to promote change in the power structure through lobbying at a higher level.
3) *'Ten-Minute Theatre – Breaking the Chains,* with workshop, was for schools and other interested audiences in the UK, supporting the 'Cancel the Debt Campaign'. The aims were to educate on issues of development and debt, raise awareness and promote active support to help the Bangladeshi people become more active in their own lives. It put the case for personal involvement and community action.

The set

A touring show to be performed in any space approximately 15x15ft to an end-on audience. Projection screen stage left. Corrugated masking flats upstage. Musical instruments stage right, two chairs. The audience needed to recognise a number of locations. These were projected onto the screen, e.g. Chairman's Office. Costume and simple props also reinforced location.

Genre and style

Epic structure; *representative* acting; visual storytelling as sketches were in Bengali; minimal set and props, moved freely from location to location; *montage* of scenes showing problems and responses.

Breaking the Chains – The Story of Land: Working for Rice.

Forms and devices

Projected images gave words of songs, information on debt, actors as workers sat in audience; points made explicit by interrupting action with direct address; songs; audience participation; impersonal narrator gave additional factual information; actors played multiple roles. Bangladeshi musicians and singers started and ended piece. Factual information was given on Third World debt followed by a series of sketches showing incidents in village life.

Description of performance action

The show opened with musicians performing a beautiful traditional song. The words in Bengali were projected, inviting participation. An English-accented narrator gave factual information for reasons behind poverty in developing countries, supported by slide projections.

A young British/Bangladeshi performer, Sujel, with a Luton accent, arrived late and walked through the audience complaining loudly that the play had started, like a worrying audience member. He then walked on stage, saying, 'That's my cue', and played a doctor. There followed a series of sketches showing causes of oppression and ways of working in teams to effect change. A section of translated script is given to demonstrate the style. Sujel's comments are in English.

LOTA AND MUSICIANS   Song

SUJEL   (*comes in late and sits in audience*) So we've started.
             I must have missed part of it. (*Generally heckles.*)
             (*Projected Image: 'Location: house of Sakina and Akkash'.
             Sakina enters with pitcher which she puts on floor and starts
             sweeping. She is clearly unwell and falls, grasping her head,
             to the floor.*)

SUJEL   (*to audience*) She doesn't look too well.

AKKAS   Sakina! Sakina! (*Looks at audience.*) Aunt come fast – Sakina
             is lying senseless on the floor. (*Aunt comes through
             audience, general panic and Sakina is carried off.*)

SUJEL   (*to audience*) What's this about debt? I mean if you've
               borrowed money, you've got to give it back. Cancel the debt,
               how do we know that's going to help the poor?
               (*Image: location: 'Doctor's chamber'. Akkas enters hastily.*)

AKKAS   Doctor, doctor, my Sakina is severely ill. Come with me
               now.

SUJEL   Oh, that's my cue. Got to go. (*Walks on stage.*)

DOCTOR   Where is the money for my treatment? No Taka? No money,
               no treatment.
               (*Akkas fumbles in his pocket, he has no money. He does not
               know what to do. With a purposeful expression he realises
               he can pawn his land to the chairman if he submits the
               documents of ownership. Doctor exits SL, Chairman enters
               SR, sits on a chair, chews betel-nut, and reads a newspaper.
               Akkas enters with his document of land entitlement. Image:
               location: in front of Chairman's house.*)

AKKAS   Ashalamu Alayaikum, Chairman Shaheb.

CHAIRMAN Walaiku Masalam.

AKKAS   My Sakina is seriously ill. Here is the document of my land.
               Please give me some money.
               (*Unwillingly he gives the document. Chairman takes it and
               nestles down on the chair again.*)

CHAIRMAN How much do you need?

AKKAS   Five thousand!

CHAIRMAN Two thousand!

AKKAS   Four thousand!

CHAIRMAN Three thousand!
               (*Akkas thinks then shakes [as is the custom in Bangladesh]
               his head in agreement.*)

CHAIRMAN Kodduce (*Directs Kodduce to get a thumb print as signature on a document. Chairman shows himself counting two and a half thousand rupees.*)

SUJEL (*to audience*) Poor fella, he thinks he's loaned his land but he's sold it. Aren't you glad you can read?
(*Image: location: house of Sakina and Akkash. They are brutally evicted by the landlord's men because they nolonger own it.*)

ANONDI (*to audience*) With a Health Service and schools, they would not be landless. Sakina would have had free health care, and Akkash would have read the document but the Government has to pay back debts. ...

SUJEL (*to audience*) It's hard working when you haven't got a voice.
(*Image: eight slides show the villagers working in groups saving together to secure a small piece of land.*)

At the end of the show, after the song, and before the audience clapped, Sujel made a direct request to the audience to give an hour of their time every week to help the poor.

The process of creation

There is a strong Theatre in Development movement in Bangladesh whose purpose is to educate villagers through didactic performances. Passe Partout were invited to initiate a performance style with a wider scope. The intention was to connect the people in the poorest villages with those making decisions at government level. The theatre piece they presented had to confront the prejudice that it is only the ill-educated who learn from theatre. Passe-Partout aimed to create a performance piece which informed all levels of society about the conditions faced by the poorest. They were funded to work alongside grass-roots organisations who work closely with villagers.

Michèle Young, Passe-Partout's Artistic Director, and company member Ruth James flew to Bangladesh and spent four weeks with the team researching and developing the initial piece. They worked alongside the host organisations to share their practice and methodology and ensure the three groups were working towards the same aims. Together they recognised three potential audiences and thus three potential programmes: firstly a direct education and empowerment programme for the villagers; secondly an information and lobbying programme for Bangladesh officials, and broader education about debt issues and thirdly specific support from European audiences. Their starting point was to create a theatre based project in which the views of the villagers would be represented.

Week 1

The research team included four leaders from the women's groups. They collaborated on drawing up questions. These were then discussed with each committee for improvements and additions. An interview day and time were agreed for all members.

There was basic training in interview techniques. Interviewers were asked to improvise bad discussions, for example, sitting on a chair while the interviewee sat on the floor; wearing make-up, or holding pen and paper: these are all symbols of inequality. The importance of establishing intentions was also emphasised; some villagers thought they were bringing money, not self-responsibility.

Creating the questionnaire: the first workshop: as Bangladesh is an Islamic country, men and women worked in separate groups. The emphasis was on breaking down barriers and exploring what was learnt from games and improvisations. Simple circle games were played such as ordering selves in order of height, or alphabetically. This developed into *Fruit Bowl*. *Fruit Bowl* became a truth game with statements that expressed feelings about arriving for the project, e.g. 'I feel anxious.' Statements developed into instances of injustice; shared expressions were about how it made them feel, e.g. 'Bribers make me angry.' Statements moved to larger causes of injustice – causes such as illiteracy or slavery. The group gave local examples, and after lunch moved to regional, then national levels. The twelve participants then divided into groups. Each group produced twenty questions. Other groups tested the questions and the best were chosen for trial in the villages.

Research in the villages established six possible answers for each question. This method of research helped ensure the end product would be based on proven research, rather than a series of exaggerated stories. Examples of questions and possible answers:

How do the powerful escape punishment?
Power of money
Lack of laws
Lack of awareness
Lack of unity
Lack of skills
Other

Why the poor who stand for vote in the elections cannot win
Scarcity of money
Manipulation of the influential
Social unawareness
Lack of advertisement
Lack of unity
Other

Interviewers would also collect accounts of events which would form the basis of the drama. Committee members were invited to add questions.

Week 2

400 village people were interviewed through a ten-minute 'chat' style approach. Interviewers then filled in questionnaires giving factual data and accounts of instances of injustice.

Analysis of the questionnaires: the quantitative data was made into statistical charts. Performers started to improvise, taking the most commonly experienced accounts of injustice as starting points. For example, in the village of Chonkali: the landlord's men stole the women's fish and attacked the women. One girl was held by her hair and ducked in the pond. She couldn't see for six months. There was a fight. A landlord's son set village houses on fire. The villagers beat him and tried to take him to the police. The landlords returned to rescue him. The next day the police arrested the villager who led the protests against the landlords – the charge was made up.

Postscript to this story: an indicator of the project's success was that one year after the play was shown in Chonkali, eight acres of Kash land had successfully been reclaimed. The village children still perform the play.

Groups selected stories to develop dramatically. Each group chose the answers that created the most complete story. Time was spent exploring and establishing a common language of theatre and drama. There was anxiety about showing real people's suffering and the impact in the villages. Participants agreed the audience needed to feel the pain so they could recognise the injustice which caused it, then think and want to change things.

The scripts were written collectively. Performers mimed their work to the director who shaped the pieces into effective dramatic statements aided by an interpreter.

Week 3

The third week was spent fusing material into a single frame and script. Ways of interacting with the audience were explored, principally through using the questions to prompt responses. Interaction would also be invited through direct address and humour. Questions would be asked and the opinions given by the previous audience shown through a human graph. The structure was discussed collectively, and final refinements were made by Michèle. They decided to call it *The Story of Land* as without land there is no security.

Week 4

Field testing in the villages with immediate response 'chat' questionnaires: 'How did you feel about the drama?'; 'Was the evening enjoyable?' 'Give details of what worked well and what didn't.' There was useful feedback, for example, an instance of a woman being ducked was inaccurate, and there were problems in the facts reported from the village of Chonkali. 20% of audiences had never seen this type of drama before. Villagers were genuinely moved to see their own stories performed. They wanted to see the rationale of the 'influential' people more fully represented. In discussion they agreed to use some dramatic licence for the purpose of moving the audience to feel and think. The piece was developed accordingly. A polished performance was shown to an invited audience in Dhaka whose feedback was far more specific, e.g. 'Sit up quickly on entrance of Lota.' The work was almost finished. A final evaluation questioned the balance between comedy and tragedy. Would beating women be seen as an injustice if the audience laughed?

The piece was adapted to accommodate an English speaking audience and six of the performers flew to Britain bringing another dimension to the project. For audiences they brought ancient artistic traditions, and a rare insight into the lives of those who do not travel, other than through the eye of the Westerner's camera lens. The go-between was Sujel, whose Luton accent and confident air established a rapport with the audience. The concept was that of money and debt. Pre-performance work packs on, for example, Third World Debt were provided, which teachers could opt into on a number of levels. 'Ten-Minute Theatre – Breaking the Chains' was offered to schools at a cost of £1.00 per minute. The performance was followed up by workshops from twenty minutes in length. These ranged from debates on local action to exploration of traditional Bangladeshi culture.

The project is still developing, in Bangladesh with the original twelve performers, and in Britain with *Passe-Partout* and those centres who made a commitment to the people represented in the play.

Summary

Passe-Partout have a clear educational directive to inform and empower their audience. In *Breaking the Chains*, they also bring nations together in a shared culture of theatre.

Questions

- Which methods documented in the excerpt do you think would be most effective in changing attitudes and behaviour?

- Consider if you might want to create a piece which is influenced by cross-cultural issues and how you might set this up.

- How might Passe-Partout's methodology be adapted to explore issues in a community you know or are interested in?

- Consider the value and effectiveness of interaction between performers and audience.

4 Tomorrow's Artists: Student Devisers' Case Studies

This chapter presents the work and process of two student devising groups. The first is offered as a model of good practice. The second needs your interaction to enable it to meet its potential.

Set aside approximately three hours for the first, and two and half hours for the second case study. In both cases the work can be developed.

Suffering and the Supreme Being

An ambitious psychiatrist/journalist gets more than she bargained for after intervening to save a boy's life. A morality tale. *Suffering and the Supreme Being* is a model of good practice.

- Practical interpretation of script – 90 minutes
- The rehearsal process – reading can be done independently in preparation for the following workshop
- A practical workshop – 90 minutes.

Aims: to explore fate, chance, causation and free will. The students wanted the audience to question the values of society, asking, 'Is this how we should live?' The piece also takes on insiders and outsiders, guilt, control, motives for action, selfish and selfless behaviour, and touches on death and afterlife. There were two boys and five girls.

World of the play: Britain 2000, an asylum for the insane, and heaven.

Performance space: drama studio with full blacks creating multiple opportunities for entrances and exits. Seating capacity 60.

Set: the audience needed to recognise the space functioning as a variety of locations. It was also important they felt implicated as insiders or outsiders in the action. The audience sat end on. A line of audience members sat stage right and stage left in the performance space. Atmosphere and environment were created by lighting and devisers.

Target audience: friends, family, other students; an exam piece.

Genre: a condensed tragedy (see p. 113).

Form and devices: episodic framework; fractured narrative presented through eight scenes which elide into each other. A range of devices drawn from different genres, including surreal and stylised action, naturalistic acting, sound montage, choreographed choral movement, and tableaux. *Protagonist* for audience to identify with, versus choral society; other devisers play multiple roles. Repeated motif, direct address, and media interview for multiple responses. (*They really did use all these techniques!*)

Taped sound effects: train noise; background asylum noise.

Lighting: basic washes to emphasise the atmosphere – blue/cold for asylum/clinical scenes, yellow for warmer more naturalistic interactions; train created by flashes and taped sound effects.

Narrative structure

Prologue introducing themes of materialism and self-interest and the psychiatrist's prophetic Dream.

Moves into **Ward Scene** in a mental asylum and the inhabitants of a society who could not conform to its authoritarian, capitalist values.

Scene 2. A school boy is fooling round at a station and falls – the psychiatrist steps in to save him and falls to her death.

Scene 3. Heaven: the psychiatrist is dead but, believing it is her right to control her life, pleads for a chance to return to earth to prove herself right.

Scene 4. Elide back to falling scene, which is replayed – this time the boy falls.

Scene 5. Media interview witnesses. (*Dead boy ties a rope to his wrist and the psychiatrist's; he is attached to her.*)

Scene 6. Psychiatrist's associates make clear she has changed. She has withdrawn and talks to herself. They think it's because she is working with mental patients. Psychiatrist and dead boy tied to her are visible on another part of the stage showing audience the reason for her withdrawal is her burden of guilt.

Scene 7 (Church). Chorus speak psychiatrist's thoughts as she recognises her error, and begs to be rid of her burden and die. A voice tells her she is damned to eternal bondage for taking her choice.

Scene 8 (Ending). Psychiatrist has become a patient in the mental asylum.

Excerpts of script and analysis of meaning – group directed reading

The play was scripted towards the end of the rehearsal period. Four scenes are reproduced below to show how meaning was created through a range of dramatic techniques.

After warming up – falling and lifting exercises are a good foundation for physical work – you should work practically on the material in groups of four to seven.

To recognise the impact of the interplay of *forms* in a meaningful way, read the script aloud in groups of 4–7, casting yourselves as Psychiatrist and actors 1–6; you may have more than one role. Follow the stage directions and enact as fully as possible. Discuss the statements and questions at the end of each scene.

LX indicates a change in atmosphere or location. Sound cues are indicated by SX. One member should read stage directions and cues. Action is interpreted in **bold italics**. SL and SR mean stage left and stage right.

Prologue

House lights down. Cast members sitting amongst audience indistinguishable from them with minimal costume. Each starts to whisper a monologue which gets louder and louder until LX1 Psychiatrist comes centre stage facing audience with direct address, posing questions which are treated in the play.

PSYCH Yes, my last two books were extremely successful.

(Starting speech demonstrates her control, and that she is an 'insider'.)

Following speeches overlap.

ALL Right, right, right? (*pause*) Or wrong?

6 People believe they are normal.
5 That they are moral and right.
4 They believe that they are in control.
3 That they can make their own choices.
2 People are blinded by their own interest.
1 They do not need to open their eyes.

PSYCH But what happens when fate takes control? What happens when life becomes an accessory? When dream and reality merge, which is real? What happens when the consumer won't buy the bargain of the day. When the empty billboard only reflects the filthy pavement slabs, the tombstones of today.

LX2; SX1 *Dream motif*
     Sound montage with voices; dim lights reveal characters 1–6 on stage, facing audience on three sides with expressions of grief, desperation, hysteria, smugness, searching, and panic. They are drawn as by a magnet to centre stage where Psychiatrist stands. They pull her, she tries to escape. She has blank eyes and a smile. A spotlight comes up on her centre stage. They lift her in the air, pull her over, squash in, pull her out in a spiky shape, intertwine, putting Psychiatrist on ground, rise slowly and reveal her in a twisted, death position. Freeze.

LX3 *Image of death.*

Aims for Prologue: it was the Psychiatrist's (protagonist's) job to intimidate, oppress, and cause grief to the other characters. Yet she needed to be real for the audience so they would empathise. Her inner consciousness was conveyed through the dream – being torn apart. The audience should connect with her self-torture.

Ward Scene

LX4; SX2
(PSYCHIATRIST *seated, drops folder, startles, gasps and wakes up.*)

6	(*warder*) Sssh. It was only a dream.
PSYCH	I'm fine. I just need to get on with the interviews.
6	(*passing dictaphone*) Try not to upset them today.
PSYCH	Yes. Well, I have to get my book written. The government wants these cases explored and I'm not here to waste time and money. Besides, there's not many people that would come here, you know, put up with their uncontrollable behaviour. (*Reflects*) I just want to get out of here as quickly as possible. If they get upset, you take control. That's your job.
6	Well. The government put them in here.
PSYCH	What? The only thing that put them in here was their own minds, their own actions. They chose to go against society, they didn't want to conform. Then they complain when they're put in here. (*Shakes head in disrespect. Into dictaphone*) Notes for chapter 5, *The Authorised Mental Science Handbook*, interview with patients 2.54 p.m., Day Room, South Wing. (*To patients*) I am here to assess your behaviour. It is in your own interests to co-operate and I would advise you to do so. The warden will be present at all times.
1	If we talk will you listen?
2	Or should we put on masks to secure your ignorance?
PSYCH	What do you mean?
1	What do you care? How much value are we to you? Life is cheap.
PSYCH	To you maybe.
2	Are you prepared to break down your assumptions? We may be prisoners here, but you're a prisoner of your own mind.
PSYCH	Your dysfunctional behaviour has been of no use to society. Your attitude led to your confinement, don't you understand?
1	It's you that do not understand.
PSYCH	I'm not here to try and understand your problems. Only assess them. (*pause*) You do know why you're here?

The movement is from everyday speech to a choral, heightened, metaphysical questioning which connects to the deeper meaning of the play, fate and destiny.

/ indicates overlapping speech.

3	What do you hope it will be? A boy or a girl? Or neither? My Mum hoped for that, she wanted to keep it a secret. She said, "Other people fall on their feet, but you just fall on your back with your legs wide open/
PSYCH	(*into dictaphone*) /Promiscuous lifestyle/
3	/I thought she was joking when she said she'd send me away – until they came to get me. She certainly never meant for me to come back/
PSYCH	(*into dictaphone*) Disowned by Mother/
3	/She burnt my bed, burnt everything. I didn't care. I just couldn't stand the stares when they escorted me away. The way people treat you and the way they look at you. The way they hate you and the way they blame you/.
PSYCH	/(*into dictaphone*) No understanding of authority.
3	/Everyone blames me but I never cried.
PSYCH	/(*into dictaphone*) Emotional imbalance/
3	I looked at it before they took it away and I thought, you bastard, you lucky bastard. Dying is a blessed release/.
PSYCH	/(*into dictaphone*) Lacking basic maternal instinct/
3	/How much better it would have been if I had been born like that. With a cord around my neck.
PSYCH	(*into dictaphone*) Conclusion, deviant lifestyle leading to mental instability. Possible cause for breakdown, guilt, self pity.

The girl's broken monologue is misinterpreted by the Psychiatrist, the audience feel pity for the girl, and establish the distance of the Psychiatrist from the patients. However, the Psychiatrist maintains a real persona.

2	Who are you to judge us?
PSYCH	Speak up. I can't hear you.
1	Can't or won't? You only hear what you want.
5	But do you hear right? Do you hear the sound of a train?
PSYCH	My dream?
4	Or your reality? What if we only exist in your dream?
PSYCH	Dreams mean nothing. I've proved that in my studies. They're a simple process for cataloguing thoughts.
4	So you've been told.
PSYCH	So that's your excuse, fate. I didn't realise people still believed in it.

2	You can't imagine what it's like in here. Choking inside with rage, frustration, and bitterness – then to be put on display for the likes of you.
PSYCH	Isn't there room for anything in your mind but prejudice and fear?
6	You block your ears and you shut your eyes. Doesn't anything matter to you beyond your own reflection in the mirror?
	(*Warden tries to sedate patients – huge struggle.*)
4	I'm not afraid of you, it's you who are afraid of me. Dreams show you what you cannot face.

The background of an asylum gives an uneasy edge to the patients' words – are they only the words of the mad? They set the action rolling, reminding the audience of the first dream sequence and the Psychiatrist's vulnerability. It also starts to build tension.

5	I have dreams, I have such dreams. He'll cut my throat if I tell a lie.
PSYCH	Tell the truth then, tell me the truth
5	Afterwards I went to him.
	(*One patient crying, three others rocking on floor, one walking around stage uncomfortably near audience.*)

Script cut here.

	Psychiatrist records patient's monologue (actor 5)/
PSYCH	(*shrugs off*) Earlier beliefs confirmed. Mentally unstable. (*Turns to go.*)
1	You think because we are different …
3	You pretend you have a future. Stop fooling yourself. Your future and mine are one and the same.

Begin train noises as Psychiatrist turns to chair for her bag etc. All walk over stage in choreographed pattern until Psychiatrist turns to go – inmates struggle after her – she exits through audience. Inmates are left in a grotesque tableau reaching after her.

SX	
LX	*Black out.*

Aims for Ward Scene: to present characters with believable situations in an insane asylum. Audience to recognise their sanity as opposed to society's harsh judgements. The Psychiatrist interviews patients who are

pitiful and desperate, making heartless judgements. They shuffle and twitch, each with their own idiosyncrasy.

Questions

- How does the language of the individual characters draw the audience's sympathy or otherwise?

- What performance styles should be employed to ensure the aims are met?

Scene 3 – Train Scene

On stage devisers 2, 5, and 6 waiting along a straight line looking into audience stage right as for a train. Psychiatrist enters, walks SR–SL.

PSYCH	Thank God I'm out of there.
5	I hope it's not late.
6	I wonder.
2	What about?

Enter devisers 1, 3 and 4 as school children aged around 15.

Creates visual interest and expectancy by different groups entering.

1	What time's the train gonna be here?
3	In about ten minutes.
1	Hey. What about Mr Johnston today?
4	What about Mr Johnston?
1	He had a right old go.
4	Yeah, well, it was all your fault.
1	He should have written the work up on the /board.
4	/He did, you just didn't copy it down. You got what you deserved.

The content and simplicity of the dialogue establishes the characters, a recognisable group of children messing about. The audience know them – likeable, innocent, funny with a life ahead. The scene then swiftly moves into its subject – and the tension builds rapidly – this piece has a lot of ground to cover in 25 minutes.

1	Just shut up.
4	You shut up.
1	Oh look, I'm close to the edge, might fall in but ohhhhh no.
3	Stop it. Get away from there.
4	Stop pratting about.
1	Come on, Andy, let's do what we did that time before.
4	Go on then.

4 holds 1 as he leans backwards. He then does it one-handed. They freeze.

PSYCH	Stupid kids.
5	That sort of thing kills people.
6	Where are their mothers?
2	I wish they'd get back from the track.
LX6	*Train*

Devisers 1 and 4 unfreeze, and spin back to their original positions on the 'platform'.

1	Come on. Let's do it again.
3	No! Stop it, guys.
4	I don't want to do it anymore.
1	Come on!

Deviser 4 holds 1 as he leans backwards, they do it one-handed. Deviser 1 shouts out. Freeze.

PSYCH
and 2,
5 and 6 He's going to fall!

Deviser 4 pulls deviser 1 up again and they spin round to face audience.

1	Come on, one more time.
4	I've had enough. It's getting dangerous.
1	Come on.
4	No.

Deviser 4 walks to SL. Deviser 1 wobbles, about to fall. All devisers *shout* 'FATE'. *Psychiatrist grabs deviser 1 and they spin round changing places. SX3; LX7. Everyone tries to grab Psychiatrist. Then she is lifted up and pulled around (Dream Motif). She is put in a twisted shape on the ground.*

This scene plays with the audience's expectations. The acting is stylised so the audience is prepared to accept the 'freeze' conventions. The freezes push the audience into thinking the boy will fall, raising tension. They don't want anyone to fall. When the psychiatrist falls it's almost a relief. There is no longer a need to worry about whether the dream will come true. This is the first climax.

The aims of this scene are to draw the audience quickly into questioning the nature of fate, and the fine line between life and death.

Questions

- How do the devisers ensure the audience will engage with the questions?

- What is the relationship between physical control and building tension?

- How effective is the combination of natural dialogue with stylised movement?

Scene 7 – Church Scene – the second climax

Chorus have spiralled around Psychiatrist and boy, who are kneeling downstage centre. Chorus in semicircle upstage. One by one they walk down, and kneel in the space performing their prayer rituals. Thoughts are spoken in Psychiatrist's ear. The whispering builds throughout, climaxing in a sound montage at the end of deviser 4's monologue.

3	I'm so sorry. (*pause*) I'm so sorry. I know I was ignorant. I've seen what's wrong. The way people live, the way they judge. I've hurt so many, the consequences never end. The truth-tellers were there. I drugged their words.
5	Everything I've done. Everything I've seen. Everything I've learnt … It wasn't …! It was all for me – that's all there was.
2	I believe in fate. Do you hear me? I believe in fate now. I have my burden. I understand why. Everything you told me was right. I know what I am … I know what I must do – this is it.

6	I want to die now. I took what didn't belong to me – life. It wasn't his time. It was mine. I'm not the same person you saw before. Take me back – give him life, spare him the knowledge.
PSYCH	I can't live because of what I've seen, what I've done – you can't cheat reality. Once you've opened your eyes, the Dream ends. I can't live carrying the weight of this burden. I want to go back.
GOD 4	(*Psychiatrist lifts head up. Whispering intensifies, rituals expand*) You can't go back. You don't belong in heaven. Heaven is for the soul and you gave that up the second you returned to this place. You chose life over death, earth over heaven, eternal suffering over constant bliss. Fate had laid life all out and you tried to break away from this and for that you will live with the forgotten, the faithless. May no one have mercy on your soul for as long as you live, and trust me that is a very long time. You will be damned. There is no safe haven, no corner, you are alone forever with the boy as your guilt. Now go away and don't ever disturb us again or your fate will be far worse than it is now.

Psychiatrist is very distressed, trying to cut boy off. Whispering and sound montage at height. When Psychiatrist succeeds there is total silence except for her cries. When she is quiet (in position LX 13), chorus take places in semicircle around her for final scene.

Aims for Scene 7
This follows the pattern of classical tragedy. The protagonist has committed a wrong action with terrible consequences. The audience pities the Psychiatrist. They should also continue to question the nature of fate, death and life beyond.

Question

- How do you think the performance style ensured that the audience took the questions seriously?

The rehearsal process

Starting points

From the outset the students were excited by the prospect of devising their own piece of theatre. Their first action was to write what they wanted from each other. The key concept was RESPECT. By the end they had established a community of equal respect, shared aims, a good working dynamic and a mutual commitment to the task. From a given stimulus of 'fairy tales, myth and legend' the group became interested in fate, destiny, death and violence. '*We thought about things which annoyed us about the way we live, about society.*' They discussed what was exciting in theatre, film and TV – Tarantino and David Glass Mime Ensemble's *Hansel and Gretel* struck chords, the former for its wayward look at life, the latter for the way that physical actions are used to express meaning. '*We wanted to make an impact. We needed something explosive to happen on stage.*'

Rehearsal period

Eight weeks intensifying as the production date approached. The group met every day in the sixth week, but recognised it was becoming unproductive: '*We realised spending so much time and energy on rehearsing was resulting in frustrations, arguments and exhaustion! We have cut down rehearsals to three times a week plus weekends. This is more than enough as working on lines and developing characters can be done at home. If we do this, we will always be prepared for rehearsing together.*'

Research

From the second rehearsal, devisers brought in photos, images and articles that struck a chord stylistically or in content terms. These came from magazines, newspapers and other sources.

Rehearsals

'During rehearsal people would say, "Stop laughing, don't feel embarrassed." Don't say, "You'll learn, we'll teach you," it's not like that – you have to do things together.'

There was discussion to establish what devisers liked doing and what images were powerful. They agreed they liked

- lifting,
- the visual symbol of the skeleton connected to the psychiatrist,
- the thematic symbol of trains as communicators between different worlds, and
- the scary, lonely world of the individual traveller.

There was also the potential of dramatic excitement with big noise and lights.

They experimented with lifting and pulling. *'It felt like I was being torn apart.'* The Dream motif was established in the second week. It gave rise to ideas of being pulled apart, then coming back to life and seeing events repeated. Its physical, symbolic nature triggered the idea of a dream which foretold the future. It was inescapable. They liked it so much they wanted to use it again as a motif. The idea of prophecy, the inability to escape fate and thus real life enactment gave this opportunity. *Creating the physical death motif very early on was important. It gave the narrative direction and complexity. It also ensured the devisers could work in the physical styles that excited them.*

They clarified their aims. No one can escape their fate. From a very physical starting point the group set about finding a way of showing this. Initially they decided not to have a written script, as the piece would largely be told through choreographed sequences.

They recognised the need for a *skeleton structure* on which to hang ideas. Initially this involved a drug dealer and a scene in a pub. Once the structure was established they worked in a disciplined way, creating the piece scene by scene, and completing it structurally by the end of each week.

 Often clichés and stereotypes are springboards from which more sophisticated ideas will emerge.

Initially they worked on structure and physical theatre ideas. The emphasis was on showing the audience action. Later they recognised the need for words and a script. Scenes were written collaboratively. *'We wrote the script together slowly and painfully, scene by scene, again and again.'* Later, different people took responsibility for individual scenes or monologues.

They were concerned to show the vulnerable side to all characters. 'What would scare the psychiatrist was to lose control. So the beginning of the play is about her being in control, and the end is about her losing control'. Through working on the character of the psychiatrist, they recognised that, in terms of the play, people inside society are those that think they can control it.

They worked on learning lines and gathering props and costumes in a practical, business-like way.

They developed the characters for the Ward Scene concentrating on showing internal struggle through repetitive movements and gestures. The devisers wanted to establish realistic characters rather than stereotypes. They wanted the audience to see their vulnerability and sanity against the insanity of the value system of contemporary Britain. They wanted to show the internal struggles that afflicted the characters. In rehearsal, working on characters naturalistically was exposing and no one felt confident so they took personal responsibility for how characters would be communicated in performance by, for example, developing histories, monologues and working on voice and physicalisation at home. They recognised realistic characters would arise from practice and doing work to raise confidence.

The tutor was the external eye and ensured through detailed critical commentary that the narrative was clearly expressed through the action.

Some rehearsal activities for the Ward Scene

- Concentration/relaxation exercises for warm up.
- Devisers had to get into character and improvise with states of tension exercises; discovering status; defining relationships and emotions.
- In turn each was put into the centre and questioned.
- They were victimised, shouted at, blamed for their inadequacies.
- Through this they realised the inmates weren't insane but victimised, a crucial distinction in the meaning made by these characters.
- Applied understanding in developing characters physically and vocally, and action was choreographed.

Some rehearsal activities for the Train Scene

Aims: To show a cross section of society, and how a casual death affects individuals differently.

- Gave each other characters and a reaction to someone dying.
- As a **Magic If** – What would you do?
- Put responses into a visual, physical tableau. Five had the same response so these needed variation and detail.
- Everyone developed their responses through statements/monologues, which gave rise to the sound montage: the structure for the report also came from stated thoughts.
- To develop physical range and detail the devisers developed their characters' responses at home and brought them to the next rehearsal. Individual devisers also wrote their own 'interviews'.

Summary

'We had become a different group at the end. We were all passionate. We saw we were doing something of our own we really liked. We learnt to compromise.'

This devising group were keen to work in a physical way, using stylised structures in their exploration. The danger of working in this way is in having too much freedom so it's hard to find a route. In fact there was a clear skeleton structure to follow, that provided by the narrative structure of **tragedy**.

'It was incredibly hard.' The devisors worked with commitment and courage to create a piece of theatre which was trilling and disturbing to watch. They consciously explored genre and form to find new ways of expressing ideas in theatre language. They taught and learnt from each other. They were ambitious and dedicated.

A practical workshop for devising groups

This workshop invites you to work with a classical structure in a physical style.

Aims: to create three scenes of **physical theatre**

Resources: music, bring your own – slow/dreamy; hectic; threatening; sad; atmospheric. Percussion instruments.

Groups: of 5–7; if possible work together throughout.

Warm-ups: objective: feel safe about touching. Activities: physical games and balances without words; *Guardian Angels*; rocking; pushing; falling.

The devising:

- Create a physical motif without talking – with lifting, balancing, and pushing. Then discuss what story it might have told. Connect the story to your own lives and experience.
- Who is the key character in the piece? Collectively discuss what he/she wants (their *objective*). (In *Suffering and the Supreme Being* the psychiatrist's objective is to write a successful book.)
- What is going to stop them getting it? (In *Suffering* fate stops the Psychiatrist getting what she wants).
- Create a climactic scene which shows the struggle with the adversary – that which stops them. (If your protagonist obtains their objective, the play will be a 'comedy' even if it isn't funny!). First clarify characters' objectives and narrative action. Then focus on building tension.
- Discuss the resolution – what image will you leave the audience with?
- Make the opening of your piece. What style will you use to introduce the audience to the themes? Include at least three different forms, e.g. sound montage, tableau, direct address.
- Return to the motif. Clarify the physical action in relation to the narrative. Decide where to place it and how often. Try adding sounds of percussion for impact.
- Put your three scenes together and perform to an audience.
- Discuss your process and performance as members of a group, and the value of using a structure.

It is often helpful to articulate what you have achieved. The following two exercises invite you to do this. It is important to do them very quickly.

As a group imagine you are promoting your piece of theatre:

1) In five minutes: write two sentences which will sell your show. What visual image will accompany the text? Give it a title.
2) In ten minutes: Make an application for an Arts Council grant to develop your piece.
   - Say why it is important and ground breaking.
   - Discuss style and content.
   - Detail size of company.
   - State number of hours you expect to rehearse.

- State your intended audience.
- Give any other expenditure details you would incur in developing the piece, including staging and lighting needs.
- Write your conclusions in a 500-word report addressed to the Arts Council – pairs or a homework task.

Leaving Germany

(a) Participate as expert devisers in an interactive process – one hour
(b) Practical workshop, analysis and evaluation – 30 minutes
(c) Practical devising project – one hour

At the start this devising group wanted to do as well as they could. Once in rehearsal, despite best intentions, they were unable to make creative progress. The study is here because it is a familiar pattern for devising groups. As an interactive model, in some sense it is still being created; it is therefore written in the present tense. In responding you will consider:

- constructive ways of working as a group,
- tasks which would generate more varied performance material, and
- ways of making a creatively productive environment where everyone had the same aim, and carried equal responsibility.

(a) Expert devisers in an interactive process

Read aloud in your group.

Aims: To show the impact of the rise of the Nazis on individual lives.

The world of the play: 1930s Germany and 1940s Britain; the domestic life of an upper middle class German/Jewish family.

Performance space: drama studio with blacks. Seating capacity 60. End-on stage. The audience needed to recognise the space functioning as various rooms. Set and props indicated these. It was important that the company made the presence of doors and windows clear through appropriate actions.

The devising company consisted of three girls and two boys. The piece was 22 minutes long.

Target audience: friends, family, other students; an exam piece.

Genre/style: predominantly naturalistic. The audience were invited to identify and empathise with all characters. The climactic scene was stylised.

Forms and devices: five scenes in an episodic framework. Those connected with naturalistic acting, i.e. working 'as if' they were in that situation; using language with a subtext, pauses, silences, etc. Climactic scene involved stylised action as music and dancing speeded up indicating disintegration and destruction. The last scene mirrors the first.

Taped sound effects: shattering glass; Viennese waltz slurring and speeding up.

Lighting: all as for interior scenes: warm straw **gels** for evening, cooler steels for daytime. No abrupt lighting changes, rather cross fades from scene to scene.

Scene 1: (*The exposition and the inciting incident.*) A dinner party for family members. It is celebratory, as one daughter has just become engaged. The table is centre stage and actors face into the audience. There is a white cloth and silver candlesticks with lit candles. The atmosphere is warm and hopeful. A mother sits at the table head stage right. A girl, dressed age 13, another 19, and a young man same age sit behind the table. Costumes are sophisticated and fashionable 30s. They have dressed for dinner. Conversation is about Dresden, a city in Germany, and people in common. It is light, friendly and excited. The father arrives from stage right and sits at the table head stage left. He has difficult news, he has been made redundant from his job at an aircraft engineering works because he is designated Jewish. The evening is literally and metaphorically shattered by a brick coming through the 'window', a sound effect and a stone with an anti-Jew letter attached thrown from stage right. The father is the only one who moves to pick up the stone. He doesn't read the message.

Scene 2: (*An irrevocable decision is made.*) The family decide to emigrate to England. The older sister decides to stay with her fiancée who is a young soldier. The scene is built around a traditional **gestic** image. There is one chair on stage. The mother sits straight-backed in it. The father stands behind the chair, able to pace the space. The daughter kneels by the chair. The decision is clearly painful.

Scene 3: The younger sister packs, the older helps, showing a close relationship based on a happy shared past. The action revolves around selection and rejection of items. Props are very important. The audience are invited to care for the characters.

Scene 4: (*Climax.*) An empty stage on which the engaged couple dance to a Viennese waltz. It starts orderly, refined but the music speeds up, gets out of control, forces them apart and they spin wildly off the stage.

The final scene: (*Resolution.*) The mother and father sit in the same positions at table as in Scene 1. There is no cloth or silver. Their clothes are shabbier. There is little talk. The younger sister enters stage left, angry about her low status work – her job is sewing. The father has no work, and sits silent and depressed. A postman enters stage left and gives the mother a bundle of unopened letters, which the audience recognise as those written to the daughter in Germany. There is little response from the family. They are numbed by events. The mother weeps. Blackout.

Discuss: in what ways do you think the piece would be effective?

Exercise

Group discussion
Below is a summary of the rehearsal process of the student devising group who made *Leaving Germany* (footnotes appear on p. 86). Your task is to become expert *objective advisers* interacting with the rehearsals.

- Pinpoint where and how different decisions and actions would lead to creative progress.
- Focus advice and comments on actions to meet the objective of 'producing an original piece of theatre in which all have opportunity to reach their potential'. Numbers in the text are cues for you to intervene. Questions to consider are in italics at the end of each week's rehearsal.
- Make your suggestions clear statements of advice with reasons.
- Finally, compare your group's suggestions with those at the end of the chapter. The numbers in the text refer you to the appropriate comment for that point in the process.

Rehearsal Process

Week 1

Decide something practical must be done each session. Discuss ideas. All agree they would like to do a play about life in a Jewish Ghetto in 1930s Germany.[1] Two girls have Jewish ancestors. One will bring her history to the next rehearsal.[2]

Discussion:
- What should they have done in their first rehearsal to ensure good organisation and effective use of time?
- What experience do they want for their audience? What theatre language will help them achieve this?
- Having decided on this theme, what should they bring to the next rehearsal?

Week 2

Decide they don't want to play old people but people their age and younger.[3] They decide on a number of roles[4] and start to develop their characters through discussion and hotseating at a superficial level. They improvise a scene naturalistically – Nazis entering the ghetto; people hiding, scared. It creates a tense atmosphere. They are excited. It is break time. They end the rehearsal on a high.[5]

Discussion:
- What problems arose through ending rehearsal straight after an improvisation?
- How could they build on the improvisation ready for the next rehearsal?
- How could they develop their ideas through experiments with different genres and forms?

Week 3

After discussion, some focus on devising ideas; they try to reproduce the previous impro. It doesn't work, there is no atmosphere, it feels embarrassing and they are despondent. They decide to abandon that scene although it was the idea that excited them most, and potentially the climax of the piece.[6]

Discussion:
- What factors may have led them to abandon the scene?
- What attitudes might have allowed a more positive outcome?
- How might experiment with styles and forms have helped?
  What exercises have you experienced that they might have tried?

Weeks 4–5

The company is becoming anxious. They are unable to develop. They do not have a skeleton structure. Ideas are suggested and quickly abandoned. The company talk and argue a lot. Practical work is half-hearted and objectives are not clear. They continue to pursue the theme of young people together in a ghetto, but cannot find a plausible situation; most people of that time lived in families of two or three generations.[7] They still want the climax to be a mass shooting. It is hard for them to reconcile the play of their imaginations with the play they can devise together, especially as they try to work in a naturalistic style.[8] Some actors can't work seriously and keep laughing. This angers others who are working with emotional intensity, they feel vulnerable.[9] Two devisers' attendance is erratic.[10]

- What practical work could help them develop their skeleton structure? Does the mass shooting have to be at the end? Where else could it be placed?
- What stylistic elements can they bring to realise the mass shooting?
- What should they do about erratic attenders?

Week 6

Half the group have given up hope. One deviser, Liberty, is still highly driven and takes responsibility for the whole group. She seeks tutor assistance. They work out a five-scene skeleton structure with clear roles for the five devisers.[11] Liberty imposes the idea on the group, and after heated and frustrated discussions, all agree it as a way forward. Liberty organises and runs rehearsals, and buys and collects props. The company are now under performance pressure and work hard to achieve success.

Discussion:
- How could the group have organised roles and responsibilities in a different way to avoid the final week crisis?
- What role could the company have asked the tutor to play?
- Should one person direct a devised piece?

Week 8

Technical rehearsal, dress rehearsal and performance.
Scenes were devised and improvised in day and late evening rehearsals.
Liberty constructed a cue-to-cue script with lighting and sound cues
marked. Performances were committed and the audience were touched
by the piece.

(b) Exercise – prevention is better than cure

Take on the role of Expert Devisers addressing this company at an early
stage of rehearsal. For each of the following bulleted headings give *two
concrete proposals.*

- Team work and ownership
- The need for research
- Warm-ups and practical work
- Genre and form

Making a rehearsal schedule (15 minutes)

Imagine eight weeks part-time, or whatever suits your situation.

Divide a large piece of paper into a grid with eight rows down and three
columns across as below. As a group discuss what targets the group might
have set itself week by week to achieve its potential and fill in the grid.
Consider the processes of the Companies in Chapter 3.

Week No	Aims	Tasks
Week 1		
Week 2		
etc.		

Discussion and report

See devising through the eyes of an assessor: take on the role of the
group's teacher/examiner. Discuss and present a summary identifying

strengths and weaknesses in the process. Summarise discussion in a report of around 250 words.

(c) Practical devising project

The process was difficult and painful, rather than creative, challenging and empowering. *It didn't have to be like that.* This workshop takes a different approach to the initial rehearsal and establishes good practice for the rest of the process.

For the workshop to be effective, work in groups of 4–7 and imagine you are at the start of an eight-week part-time, or four-week full-time devising project. Your stimulus is *Leaving Germany.*

Resources: For recording work camcorder or tape recorder; large piece of paper for group; individual note books for ideas.

Activities – part one – generating material

Play everything at performance level. *Allow 30 minutes.*

Aim: *to* generate material for use in a devised piece.

Warm-up exercises: Peter's keys, piggy in the middle, sardines, or other hiding/hunted games. Then:

- Brainstorm Holocaust ideas
- Image/sculpt
- Add a phrase
- Evaluate through standing outside, seeing and responding one by one
- Question: *Does the image move or excite? What and who do you see, what questions can you ask? What stories are being told?*

This is material you may use later, be rigorous in breaking it down. It's your starting point. Don't dismiss ideas too quickly, there is time to explore. Then:

- Choose one deviser to take on the role of facilitator or director, stay outside, give directions below and watch.
- Others reform image, repeat phrase, while developing a rhythmical repetitive movement – there is no right or wrong way.

- Draw on discussion of images to develop 'lines' into small monologues as you start to take on the identity of another. Who are you? What are you doing? What do you want? Are you hunter or hunted?
- Facilitator turns on recorder if available, as there is potential for material for script.
- Leave the safety of the group image, *turn off any lights* and imagine self to be in another space, hunted or hunter, talking or whispering. Concentrate on creating atmosphere. If hunted, you hide; if hunter, you stalk and seek. No one is caught. Noise and movement is continuous and erratic. Find a quiet solitary space for character work with imagination.
- Facilitator feeds in questions to create detail for characters, e.g. *Who? Where? Time of day? What you want? Year and season? Physical environment? Your appearance?* It is important to visualise details of colour, texture and atmosphere.
- Freeze action, spotlight individuals, who give first-person thoughts. Be ready to record – you may get some raw, exciting material which you can transcribe. Devisers as characters, speaking in first person, share thoughts and desires (as monologues). Director can question to clarify or create more belief.
- End by stretching, yawning and shaking off roles.

Workshop strengths: your group works collaboratively, no one has more ownership than anyone else. All have the opportunity to be engaged in the creative process. You have generated 'material' from which to select in the way of *Improbable Theatre*, *Trestle Theatre* and *Northern Stage Ensemble* – situations, characters, mood and atmosphere; there will also be a number of potential narratives to follow.

Activities – part two – developing devising skills

After the workshop, evaluate outcomes. Allow around 15 minutes.

- What structures will you use in discussion to ensure everyone contributes and their ideas are valued? The discussion needs to be fair, positive and open.
- You are looking for material to develop. You may choose an ensemble scene, individual monologues or characters from the work, whatever seemed interesting. Discuss what did not work quickly and dismiss it.
- Director/outside eye recaps and shares experience.
- Each deviser shares two or three significant moments.

- Give each moment recalled a title; write them as headings on pieces of paper. These are your 'stories'. Set aside for development later.

Activities – part three – developing the piece

If you are excited by your progress, develop your piece. Establish how much time you can give over the next two weeks. Decide aims, objectives and how to progress. Limit discussion to five minutes or less for each task.

- Where can you go from here? Create a skeleton structure.
- Consider theatre styles – what's excited you from theatre, film or television. For inspiration and practical know-how, choose a particularly strong image/style and describe how it was created on stage. Can you use any of these in your piece?
- Brainstorm research possibilities (think of buildings – war museums, memorials; people with stories; places with significance – graveyards; art works, etc. Visits give a different sort of information from that found in books. Everyone researches.
- Share tasks for next rehearsal. Be clear about what you need to bring – research/props/ideas for warm-ups. Include work generated from practical session, e.g. transcribing tapes if language or action are exciting. Individually, make sure you have a job to do.

Activities – part four – further practical work

Aims: to experiment with theatre language.

Using the given narrative, rework the introduction and one other scene outlined in *Leaving Germany*. Choose a specific and different genre for each. Include at least three different devices/forms in each scene.

Summary

In this chapter you have explored structures, experimented with the language of physical theatre, analysed reasons for a group not progressing, and considered how to use a stimulus to develop a broad set of responses.

Comments on the *Leaving Germany* rehearsal process

[1]First they need to establish ground rules; agree a rehearsal schedule; exchange telephone numbers; set up a company journal for recording

progress, and individual journals too. After agreeing themes, all should research historical background and bring documentary information, rather than relying on own knowledge and experience. What comes from the outside adds truth, depth and complexity. Start to establish performance aims and objectives.

[2]The girls' Jewish history may lead to a problem of unequally owned work, because they have a vested interest in the piece. It has touched their lives. All devisers need to bring something to the next rehearsal to ensure parity, a story, an article, a response. Where does Holocaust touch each of them?

[3]Ghettos containing only young people would be most unusual. The company needed to think creatively about what situation this could be. Clarification could have led to the development of a structural framework, narrative, and therefore characters and action at a suitably early stage in the process. Work would have felt productive and creative.

[4]After this they would be in a situation to develop characters in depth through hotseating and consideration of physical and vocal presentation. Then to develop a series of improvisations to deepen their understanding of character. Finally to clarify character aims and objectives within the framework of overall objectives.

[5]This group were seduced by short term pleasure and lost a real opportunity. They needed to evaluate the strengths of their rehearsal and the improvisation and make clear plans for the next rehearsal accordingly.

[6]With more confidence and knowledge they could have kept this scene, deciding to use it as a climactic moment and building other action around it. They needed to ask for tutor support to help make a realistic assessment of quality and potential for development.

[7]They need to find a stable framework which will hold the action.

[8]They could have experimented with different theatre forms – *expressionist* techniques are often appropriate for nightmarish situations when naturalism can't deliver the goods.

[9]You can't work to capacity if you feel laughed at. Respecting intentions and group integrity is important in building confidence and belief. In such situations laughter usually arises from insecurity.

[10]A successful rehearsal may remedy attendance caused by lack of ownership, direction and motivation. In a professional company they would be sacked, but that's not usually an option in student groups. Imposing sanctions which ensure attendance is difficult. In this situation it should be a commitment to achieving a unique and exciting piece of theatre which throws new light on your subject, and a desire to achieve potential for an exam. Commitment is a question you must consider in setting ground rules. Don't be lenient.

[11]Because it was very late, students were relieved to have a structure to work to. With a clear aim and objectives they were able to put a piece together. If the group had been able to recognise and use the strengths of performers earlier, they might have enjoyed the creative process.

5 Building a Successful Team

> 'Listen to each other with care and thought'.
> 'Treat each member of the group with respect and equality'. (Devisers on devising)

The dynamic of a group is the key to either enjoying the process, or struggling to success. This is true in all walks of life. However, a devising group working creatively under pressure is a particularly delicate species, with a fragile and volatile membership. It needs to be nurtured. This chapter presents techniques for healthy growth, and warns of potential hazards. In it we will consider positive attitudes and their relationship with positive language; how devisers may discover their roles in a team; and strategies for dealing with problems that groups may come up against.

Set aside approximately 90 minutes for this workshop.

Positive Attitudes, Positive Language

Try to be open to the exercises, not guided by the analysis you may have already read a page or so on. Perhaps you could choose a facilitator to set up the work.

Getting ready to work – The impact of words

The most important thing is to like each other – do this through being nice to each other. Being creative means being vulnerable – trying out things you don't know you can do. In a supportive framework you'll go a long way. In a critical framework you'll clam up. Being supportive means building on what was good, and quickly dismissing what wasn't. That's much more difficult than the other way round.

Exercise 1 – Nice and Nasty

Group sits in circle. *Round 1*: One person begins by insulting the person on their left. **The insult must be untrue.** The person receives their insult by saying 'Thank you' and nothing more. No one else speaks. Then the person who was insulted, insults the person on their left. **The insult must be untrue.** Continue round the circle. Discuss feelings and responses.

Even though they were lies it probably felt uncomfortable.

Round 2: One person begins by saying something nice about the person on their left. **It must be true**. The person receives their compliment by saying 'Thank you'. No one else speaks. After a round, discuss feelings and responses – the power of words to hurt in combination with our vulnerabilities and sensitivities.

Round 2 is a good exercise to start rehearsals with.

Exercise 2 – Blocking and accepting

To establish the principle of working an idea. An improvisation game developed from *Keith Johnstone's Impro*. Blocking an improviser means rejecting an offer which would develop action, for example: (a) Your arm looks bad; (b) Yes, it's an old injury, do you want to see; (c) No. The final no is a block. Action doesn't happen because of it. The pair have to start on a new task.

Two players are given a situation, e.g. mending a car. A either blocks or accepts, B mends the car. One watcher tells A when to block or accept.

The discovery is that improvisers block each other all the time, often with seemingly funny one-liners that kill off the improvisation or make it hard to build it again. When the creative possibilities of accepting have been discovered, there is of course much scope for creative blocking. This work helps develop a language to clarify how you feel about what others say and do, and why you feel like that – an important element in managing group dynamics.

Exercise 3 – A language for constructive criticism

Practise saying: 'That's a good idea, what if ...?', 'Yes, and ...', 'You were good!', 'I wish I'd thought of that', etc.

Exercise 4 – The dynamics of a successful group

Groups of 4–7 devise the opening of a play in naturalistic style. Include one sound effect. Characters must reveal who they are, where they are, and their relationship to each other. Share the pieces to finish the process.

This exercise explores the process of making.

Consider your own and others' roles:

- Did anyone block or accept?
- Did everyone listen?
- Was anyone unheard?
- Was the outcome successful?
- Did your group use time well?
- Did anyone take a leadership role?
- Did anyone else want it?
- Did anyone feel responsible for completing the piece?
- Was anyone a diplomat?

Discovering Team Roles

Analysing team members' roles is a serious and profitable business. Meredith Belbin has studied team function for over 25 years, most recently at the Industrial Training Research Unit 'laboratory' at Cambridge. He has identified the individual roles crucial to a successful team and developed psychometric tests to identify different personality types. The point is that people are different and need to be allowed to function in different ways. Not everyone in a devising team can be a leader; indeed a group of leaders would find success hard to achieve. However, all can have necessary roles, what Belbin calls 'personality team roles', and often more than one. Belbin lists eight roles needed for a fully effective group. These have been reduced to seven and slightly adapted to fit the demands of a devising group.

Exercise 1

Individually read the indicators for the roles and list that or those you most closely identify with.

The Chair: co-ordinates team's efforts. Need not be brilliant or creative, but would rather be called disciplined, focused and balanced. Talks and listens well. A good judge of people.

The Shaper: highly strung, outgoing and dominant. The task leader, and if there were no chair they would leap into the role, though they may not perform it well. Their strength lies in their drive and passion for the task, but they can be oversensitive, irritable and impatient. They are needed as a spur to action.

The Plant: introverted but intellectually dominant. The source of original ideas and proposals, very imaginative and intelligent. Can be careless of details and may resent criticism. Needs to be drawn out or will switch off.

The Objective Evaluator: Analytical rather than creative intelligence, able to see the flaws in arguments. Often less involved than others. Dependable but can be cold and tactless. Might this be the role you want a tutor to play?

The Practical Organiser: Turns ideas into manageable tasks, making lists and schedules. Methodical and trustworthy, not a leader but a good administrator.

The Team Worker: a diplomatic, listening, harmonising role which holds the team together. Likeable and popular but uncompetitive. You don't notice when they're there, but miss them when they're not.

The Finisher: ensures the team meets its deadlines. The checker of details, worrier about schedules, who worries others with their sense of urgency. Their relentless follow-through is important but not always popular.

Exercise 2

After you have chosen your personality type, share findings. Find what others think about you before disclosing what you wrote.

Serious team players can investigate Belbin's work further. For us, it is enough to start to think objectively about our function in the team by naming the roles we can play, valuing them, and allowing ourselves to do them well. It's also important not to get typecast in a role – situations change and skills develop, and the structures of different groups mean different roles need fulfilling.

Exercise 3

Consider the selection of members of devising groups:

- How are your groups chosen?
- Do students choose or tutors?
- On what basis are groups made up?
- Is this an exchange you would like to take part in?
- Are there any concerns you'd like to discuss with your tutor?
- Are your reasons personal or dramatic?

Developing Problem Solving Strategies

a) Groups of 4–7 improvise different problems when devising. Work on the theme of 'Justice'. Improvisations should be spontaneous or take less than three minutes to prepare. Brainstorm examples or select from the list below.

1) The first rehearsal – problems with personalities in the group.
2) Someone is late – re-run subsequent rehearsals with the same person constantly late.
3) Midway through the process – someone has not put forward any ideas.
4) Midway through the devising process – group problems focusing on style.
5) Two days before performance – problems with commitment.
6) Two members talk horribly about a third behind their back.
7) Continuous absence due to an ill relative.
8) Rehearsal starts, three people talk about the previous evening, the others weren't there!

After each improvisation share suggestions of how the problems could be resolved. Replay the improvisation. This time the person who suggested the solution takes a role in the impro and tries to implement their solution, applying a practice from **Forum Theatre**, 'a rehearsal for life'.

These impros may well be fun. The real purpose is to share views, establish a common set of attitudes to working in a group and establish frameworks for managing problems during the devising process.

b) The second stage of preparation is to discover strategies for working positively. Each group takes their first improvisation and works it positively. Everyone is nice, says 'Yes' to each other's ideas and enacts them enthusiastically. This may be turn out rather 'cheesy' but it will show what working in a positive environment can be.

c) Build a spontaneous improvisation on justice using the skills of 'blocking and accepting'. Analyse your process in the most positive way. If you performed you achieved an outcome.

Last Thoughts

This chapter invites you to explore and reflect on the nature of individuals working in teams. Consider these questions:

• What qualities and skills will you bring to your devising group?

• Are there any attitudes or habits you might like to change?

6 The Rehearsal Process: Model Frameworks

This chapter includes:

- some advice on structuring your work;
- a rehearsal schedule model;
- useful forms;
- advice from students who have devised.

To rehearse is to move through a process of shaping and refining a concept into a complete dramatic statement. It is a constant process of decision making and creation. Making too many decisions is exhausting. Drawing on established structures frees energy for making decisions which will make your piece unique.

Structuring Time

In devising, time becomes a shapeshifter, a spirit whose quality changes according to the perspective of the viewer. Make sure it is your prisoner, not you its! Time controlled is an ally. It shows what you can achieve in a week or a month. It tells you if you're off schedule. It says when rehearsals start and end. It is a clear boundary between working hard and time out. Left to its own devices though, it becomes deceptive, sneaking unseen towards production. Then performance dates loom from the shadows, panic arises, and suddenly times darts ahead with devisers rushing madly to catch it up.

Remember – managing time means doing things logically.

Model of a Rehearsal Schedule

The next section suggests how you might use time over an eight-week rehearsal period. The Framework suggests which tasks might be done when. Blow it up and adapt it to suit your purposes with highlighters, ticks and colour coding, as production dates approach. A structured framework with tasks and objectives planned will free you into a creative and productive devising experience.

Pre-rehearsal

Establish lighting and sound possibilities

Sound effects

- Live sounds are better than recorded sounds – can any be made off stage?
- If you need special sound effects make sure they are available as soon as you know you want them.
- What recording equipment is available? There's no point having CDs if there is no CD player.
- Who will operate the equipment?
- Sound effect tapes and CDs are available from good music stores.

Lighting

The first function of lighting is to light actors and set so they can be seen. After that it is used to create mood and atmosphere. Usage will depend on a) what's available, and b) the style and action of your piece. Most groups can manage with two general lighting states, and one other 'special' for effect.

Other Effects

Gobos are stencils placed in spotlights to create a shadow silhouette on cyclorama or floor. They come in many shapes. Using a gobo may enhance your setting. If you think a gobo may enhance your play, check if they are available. Other effects like lightning or a fire are also possible if there are available lanterns.

Don't: build your piece around lighting.

Do: find out what is available on the lighting rig.

Week-by-week schedule

Week 8	**_Administration_**	
	Pre-rehearsal Gather your rehearsal kit and bring to rehearsals: • A large book to record process • sheet for telephone numbers and addresses (see form 1) • large paper for rehearsal schedule (forms 3 and 4) • personal notebooks for mulling ideas and observations • forms for recording stories (form 2). _'Ensure everyone can attend before confirming rehearsal dates.'_ • Establish a rehearsal schedule – be clear about time. Be prepared to commit yourself. Plan in advance. Does anyone have space in their home? Consider meeting three times a week in early stages for sessions of 90 minutes. • Does rehearsal space need booking? • Exchange phone numbers and addresses. • Set up group notebook for recording progress, identifying problems, identifying objectives, drawing up task lists, drawing up shopping lists, etc. **_Building a team_** _'We all wanted to be directors.'_ • Establish ground rules – what do you need from each other? What do you want to give? What do you want to gain? Are you prepared to push the boat out? What conditions will enable you to give your best? Do you need to change anything about the way you work? • Do you want to allocate team functions, or rotate them, e.g. director, someone	

responsible for summing up progress, or recording key ideas and images? Do you want to use a 'talking stick' to ensure people can talk and are listened to?

- Establish skills and qualities e.g. musician, finisher, team worker, generosity.
- Consider what function you want your tutor to play, e.g. to watch, comment on and advise on technique, structure and direction; to chivvy you into producing practical work; to help you access technical equipment.
- Collect pictures, poems, newspaper, articles, objects, photos to share at first rehearsal.
- Technical considerations – Rule of thumb – Always go for less rather than more.

Set and props

- Other groups will probably be using your performance and rehearsal space. You need to be considerate.
- If you're making a set or painting scenery consider size and durability. Is there a workshop or place for construction and storage? Do you need to book it?
- If you are painting, is there a place where the objects can dry?
- If you plan different sets for different scenes, how will you manage scene changes quickly and effectively?
- If you are planning to bring in set or props, check there is a place to store them during rehearsals.
- Is there a budget?
- Establish staging possibilities – e.g. can you work in the round? Are staging blocks available? Will you be responsible for collecting and returning them?
- Can you store props and costume safely? What about bigger objects?

	• Is there access to a PC for script writing? • Is any technical equipment available for recording and use in performance? What is the borrowing procedure? **First rehearsal aims** Generate and develop ideas which excite. *'It's important to stay happy and positive, so games and relaxation exercises were a good way to warm up'.* **Starting points** • A rule of thumb: 25% talk, 75% practical. • Sharing collected artefacts. • Working with particular styles and devices. • Topics or ideas which excite or touch. • Workshop-generated ideas you want to explore in more depth. **Warm-ups** Focusing activities and energisers are important: • Practically image the topics and themes that excite you. • Create a machine. • Do a spontaneous improvisation. Establish some early objectives: work practically to achieve them.	Establish starting points for next rehearsal
Week 7 Establish skeleton structure	Research continues: visits, reading, talking to people, watching people, listening to people. Develop material from rehearsals, stories, improvisations, stylistic elements and desires, dialogue if it is effective, scenes. Experiment with structures.	Record impros on separate sheets Establish starting point for next rehearsal

Week 6 Show tutor and others two scenes Discuss in terms of impact and aims	Consider art work and design elements. Allocate tasks. Develop material for scenes – images, tableaux, sound montage, machines, character development. State aims to audience and run scenes – invite constructive feedback	Establish challenges and how to confront them
Week 5 Halfway. Establish What you've achieved so far	Clarify actor/audience relationship and use of levels. Play energiser games. Say something nice to each other. Develop material. Keep bringing in and using costume and props.	Establish objectives for remainder of rehearsal period
Week 4 Clarify technical needs	Name your play. Experiment with any effects you want to use. Step up rehearsal time. Experiment with ideas still, but start scripting your scenes and reworking them.	Make tapes, videos and other set elements
Week 3 Prepare questions for sympathetic audience	Put scenes in running order. Work on characters and situations to develop complexity. Develop script in more detail. Work with costume. Shoes and personal props are helpful. Use set and props too. Run piece to audience and note feedback.	Continue research. Detailed character work
Week 2 Present to tutor	Prepare script for technical rehearsal. Mark up SX and LX. (see *Technical Rehearsal*, p.100). Work on developing piece according to critical comment from last rehearsal. Run. Time. Check length is right.	Meet technical crew to discuss effects

Week 1 Pre-production	Make sure scene changes are slick, tight and fluid. Make sure costumes and props are in place, sound tapes made and labelled, etc. Make programmes.	Shopping, acquiring last minute items
	Technical rehearsal	
Week 0 production week	Dress rehearsals. Last minute changes and developments.	
	First performance	

Useful forms to draw or copy

1 Names and addresses of devisers

Name	Address	Phone number

2 For recording stories and improvisations

STORY TITLE: Date:

Between (characters):

Action:

Exciting dialogue/images:

Development possibilities:

3 Schedule for planning rehearsals – headings

Week	Aims	Methods and structures	Outcomes/challenges
8			
7			
6			

4 Devising planning sheet – structure and pace

Aim:

Style:

World of the play/setting:

Units /scenes /episodes	Story /narrative	Devices /forms	Climactic /moment /gest /tableaux /motif	Staging/props /costume /SX /LX	Desired audience response

Past devisers on devising

'Don't worry about chronological order at the start.'

'Research at start and carry on until the end.'

'Start with something real that touches you.'

'Make enough time to rehearse.'

'Our group have insisted on punctuality and good attendance.'

'One person can't be a leader – the others hate them. But two people can lead together."

'Helen scripted the hotel scene straight away – we didn't use it. It didn't mean anything to anyone."

'Don't take the initial themes or idea too literally.'

'Discussion and reflection is vital – in our group we used it to set the agenda and air grievances among group members. I used it particularly for my own characterisation and development.'

'I believe the best improvisation comes out of play.'

'Have a rehearsal aim – produce two minutes of script, or develop characters – it's a focus.'

'It's not a case of sitting and discussing, the cast must jump up and get on the stage.'

'Time guillotines were designed to allow each group member a fair say.'

'Appoint a diplomatic 'director' to scenes that aren't progressing.'

'You need honest appraisal.'

Summary

This chapter has discussed the importance of good rehearsal planning to ensure good use of time. It has also noted the importance of presenting sections of your piece throughout the process to your tutor and other interested students.

Questions

- What conditions might you want to establish for the presentation of work in progress?

- How might you use these structures and grids to help you plan and run your rehearsals?

- What do you think is the most useful advice offered by past devisers?

7 How to Run Technical and Dress Rehearsals

In this chapter, we will consider:

- preparing the script for technical and dress rehearsals;
- preparing the crew;
- preparing yourselves;
- how technical and dress rehearsals should be conducted.

The *technical rehearsal* is very important and needs organising properly to make the most of available time and resources. It can be complicated or not, depending on the number of lighting changes, sound effects, set changes and costume changes you have in your piece. Always go for less rather than more.

What Happens in a Technical Rehearsal?

Lighting and sound states are plotted and run in the technical rehearsal. The technical crew have responsibility for operating lighting and sound. They want to do the job efficiently and effectively. They may have four or six pieces to run in an evening. There may not be much time. It will be helpful for them to understand the gist of your piece and the mood and atmosphere you want. A dedicated technician will practise difficult changes on the board. It is your responsibility to present a script they can read. It might include the text for all scenes, or it may have gaps where improvised scenes take place. Either way, it is important they can read when to 'press the right button'. Being well prepared for your technical rehearsal is a great time saver and cuts down bad feeling.

The technical rehearsal is a place for discipline and control. One person liaises between the technical crew and other actors running the action, probably the person who prepared the script. The piece is run from technical cue to technical cue. It is important the crew write down all information in a way which enables them to translate it quickly in performance. After the rehearsal they will need time to prepare the script properly.

Planning

During the devising process, you'll recognise that lighting, sound, staging and props are integral to your performance. The technical rehearsal is the first time you'll actually be able to see how they all hold together. This is exciting. It can also be frustrating if you are not well prepared or well disciplined. You must be very clear about the effects you want created by light and sound, and be patient while your technical crew work to get it right for you. You will certainly need technical support from a lighting operator. If your show is technically complicated, you may also need people to operate sound and help with set and costume changes.

Getting ready

- Check lights are hung and focused – devisers may need to help.
- Ensure sound equipment is in place – devisers may need to help.

Devisers' jobs

- Organise hire and collection of any special effects.
- Organise operators for light and sound (if necessary). Your centre/theatre may have technical support.
- Prepare your script for light and sound operators.
- Have set and props in place.
- If you need to see backstage, check you can – place a torch if you can't.
- Organise a changing room with mirror and hang costumes there.
- For quick costume changes, have costumes on hand.
- Organise the strike (clearing the performance space and changing area after the event).

Preparing a Script

A prepared script is a script which enables stage managers and technical crew to run a show. A well prepared script holds details of lights, sounds, special effects and set changes. Once marked up, it must not leave the technical box in case it gets lost. All sheets should be identified with the production's name. In theatres it is called 'the book' or 'bible'. When preparing a script it is important to remember that the technical crew may not know your piece. Their job is to set and operate sound, light and other elements for you. They interpret it technically as a set of instructions. A well prepared script saves valuable time in the technical rehearsal. It will also reduce the likelihood of technical hitches during performance. The simpler your technical demands, the less likely they are to go wrong, and the more they will be in the devisers' control. For marking up scripts there is a useful technical shorthand for crew and devisers to use:

LX	=	Lighting/electrics
Q	=	Cue
SX	=	Sound
FX	=	Special effect
Fly/tab	=	Curtain
MX	=	Musicians
F/S	=	Follow spot
BO	=	Black out
DS	=	downstage (nearest audience)
US	=	upstage
SL	=	stage left (actors left as they face audience)
SR	=	stage right.

Here is an example of a script marked up for technical crew with a schedule of what each lighting and sound cue achieves. This is a double check to ensure the right effect has been created.

Suffering and The Supreme Being

Scene 1

LX1   ▼ *Whispered monologues, getting louder until Journalist stands centre stage and*

LX2   *closes book.*▼

                     Yes, my last two books were extremely successful. (*speeches overlap, continuing after Journalist*)

         ALL   Right, right, right? (*pause*) or wrong?

Script continues until

         PSYCHIATRIST But what happens when fate takes control? What happens when life becomes an accessory? When dream and reality merge, which is real? What happens when the consumer won't buy the bargain of the day? When the empty billboard only reflects the filthy pavement

LX3 SX1   slabs, the tombstones of today? ▼ ▼

LX4   SOUND MONTAGE WITH VOICES ▼

LX4a   DREAM MOTIF PHYSICAL SEQUENCE. FREEZE (*2 seconds*) ▼

LX5 SX3   STAND AND TAKE PLACES IN ASYLUM. JOURNALIST ▼▼ ON CHAIR (*drops folder, startles and wakes up*)

         WARDER   Shhh! It was only a dream.

Note that the lines indicate exactly where in the action the cue buttons are pressed.

Lighting levels

Setting lighting levels for a simple rig; it assumes all lights are controllable from two master switch dimmers. Dimmer A controls warm lighting, dimmer B controls cool lighting.

Suffering and The Supreme Being
Lighting cues 1–10

Cues	1	2	3	4	4a	5	6	7	8	9	10
A	0	9	0	0	0	9	3	9	0	0	9
B	0	0	0	flicker	0	0	0	0	0	3	0
Spot									6	8	0

Note 4a – late cues can be added.

LX1	House lights off
LX2	Lights up
LX3	Black out
LX4	Flickering lights
LX4a	Black out
LX 5	Lights up full
LX6	Lights dimmed
LX7	Lights up
LX8	Spot on centre – Journalist
LX9	Dim lights and spot on Journalist
LX10	Spot off. Lights up

Sound cues 1–3

SX1	Train soundtrack
SX2	Train off
SX3	Ward Background sounds

Preparing the Crew

Treat stage managers and technical crew with respect. They are working for you and may be volunteering time. You need them more than they need you. Arrange to meet before the technical rehearsal so you can:

- present your piece;
- outline the technical demands, and the mood and atmosphere you want to create;
- if possible give them a marked up copy of the script so they can be prepared for the technical rehearsal.

Backstage Preparations

- Check for any Health and Safety hazards like trailing or exposed wires, or potential sources of fire.
- Check backstage is clear for movement.
- Have a copy of the script with cues marked so devisers can move from cue to cue efficiently.
- If there are a lot of scenes, write order and necessary props and pin where it can be seen so devisers know where they are.
- Check entrances are free.
- Set the first line of audience chairs if not in place.

You are now ready to start the technical rehearsal.

During the Technical Rehearsal

Technical crew need time to find the right lights, and set and record levels so the sequence can be repeated quickly and easily. If there are tricky fades or changes, they need time to practise. It is a matter of pride in their work for technical crew to get it right. The length of the technical rehearsal will depend on the number of cues and how complicated they are. The most efficient technical rehearsals are run from cue to cue, starting with house lights off.

- Allocate one deviser to liaise between devisers and stage manager/lighting operator. They will have the final word on lighting states and sound states. They will also instruct devisers to move to new positions for important cue points. It's important for everyone to keep focused on the task – it's hard to concentrate when devisers or stage crew chat.
- Sit in the audience to see the impact of light on actors and the space. You can't see from the stage. For spots or specials devisers should note the edges of lights and should walk into them to make sure they are lit. This is something to check.
- If there are set changes in a black out, check that the crew can see – you may need to plot a new lighting cue.
- Stage crew should wear black and walk efficiently, never run.
- Changing sets: move furniture quickly and efficiently. It may be a logical puzzle to work out the most effective way to do this and need several practices to make it slick. Changing sets effectively is an art in its own right.

- Beware of black outs – audiences may think your piece has ended. Cross fades can be as effective.
- The lighting operator should practise complicated cross fades which coincide with other effects like door bell ringing.
- If there are several pieces of theatre in one event, practise getting any set on and off.
- After the rehearsal discuss the resolution of any problems and thank the crew!

Dress Rehearsal

The Dress Rehearsal has two functions:

1. It's the only opportunity to run the show continuously with all elements of theatre involved. Problems may arise that haven't been anticipated which need resolving.
2. It's an opportunity to practise getting it right and gain confidence in doing that. Try and have an audience to perform to. It's important not to break out of role or performance at any time, so you gain a sense of the shape and structure of the piece, and the demands on you as actors in role.

Ask your tutor to watch and give any last notes.

Getting ready for the dress rehearsal

- Book the dressing room, with a mirror, access to water, and drinks.
- Check costumes are complete and hang them up.
- Place costumes for quick changes.
- Do a vocal and physical warm up.

After the dress rehearsal

- Give any notes to the technical crew straight away.
- Take some time out, then return for notes. Be disciplined about time. Be receptive to notes – write them down. Don't talk while someone else is getting notes.
- Restore costume to hangers and/or set props on stage.
- Restore personal props etc.
- Tidy dressing room.

The Performance

Preparing for performance

- Arrive at least an hour before to prepare. Take some quiet time with your fellow devisers, you've come a long way together.
- Check set and props are in place, and any tapes or other equipment.
- Dress.
- Physical and vocal warm up.
- Perform and enjoy.

After performance

Strike the set, tidy props and costume, and celebrate your achievement.

Summary

This chapter shows the discipline and practicality necessary to organise and run the technical and dress rehearsals effectively and efficiently.

Questions

- Consider the implications of the time involved on the rest of your commitments.

- What are the implications of a complicated technical piece?

- What role might you like to play in these late rehearsals?

8 Structuring Stories and Rehearsal Strategies

This chapter will consider:

* structures on which to build plays;
* practitioners' rehearsal techniques.

Making theatre happen is ultimately a fusion of practical, creative, intellectual and intuitive energies. Good pieces are always time consuming, and hard work to produce. They can also bring immense satisfaction.

Dramatic Structures

Often a first discussion devising groups have is on styles and forms, and how to use and manipulate them in making theatre. Stylistic inspiration may be drawn from a range of sources – theatre, films, dreams or novels. Beneath what inspires there is an underlying structure in which *form* and content merge to make meaning. Some dramatic structures shape the narrative, others focus on form. Usually the two are inextricably intertwined.

Tragic structure (from the Greek philosopher Aristotle): the hero or *protagonist* has a problem or fatal flaw. Tension builds until the problem is confronted at the point of a new seeing. Then there is the resolution of the play. This structure is the basis of all tragic drama.

Epic structure (term used by *Brecht* to determine a particular dramatic style): takes big events like wars, or histories as its subject matter. An *epic structure* has short *episodic* scenes which move between situations and characters. Each scene is complete in itself; together the scenes make a montage – the collective impact is greater than the sum of its parts. Useful for time and place shifts, clear message, interruption by song, chorus, narrator or other non-naturalistic devices like film, projections, video, voiceovers, etc. Often used for documentary or political-message-based theatre, for retelling a story or adapting a novel.

Naturalistic structure (associated with *Stanislavski, The System* and *Method* acting): gives the illusion of real life presented on stage. Here there is a unity of time and place. The action evolves through the situations and personalities of the characters. Shifts in atmosphere and mood are presented through developments in action as presented in situation and dialogue.

Surreal structure (associated with *Artaud, Berkoff,* and *Absurdist* theatre): draws on the language of dreams in presenting a subjective world. Its devices are strongly visual, movement and sound-focused. The task is to take the audience on a journey into the subconscious. It is often very choreographed.

Classical structure: many plays draw on this structure which assumes three acts. The first act introduces the protagonist, there is an inciting incident, the protagonist is given a quest or a problem to solve. The second act ends with a climax. The third act ends with another climax, the final act resolves the action. If it ends badly, the play is a tragedy. If it ends well it is classed as a comedy. Its focus is the development of plot and tension. It can be used as a platform on which to select stories. *Suffering and The Supreme Being, Leaving Germany* and *70 Hill Lane* have this underlying structure. Good stories often follow this structure.

Street theatre: *Welfare State* are an experimental theatre company who specialise in community and street theatre. In *Engineers of the Imagination* (p. 33) advice is given on creating a piece of street theatre:

> It should be possible to conceive of a street theatre piece as a series of sculptural pictures, to draw the key frames as a strip cartoon. Put yourself in the position of someone on the top of a passing bus, glimpsing your show for a moment – at any moment. They should be able to make something out of what they see ...
> ... a jet bomber menaces a cardboard city ...
> ... a sailor is hypnotised and dreams of a ghost ship ...
> ... the death of a gluttonous fat man ...
> ... the holy fool hunts for a nest ...
>
> Although your script should be clear and simple – take a basic story to start with – it should not be simplistic. It still can, and should, work subtly, and on many levels ... A short piece, under half an hour in length, can move through many moods. It may open with up-front knockabout comedy, turn through sinister hunting and

stalking to a dramatic fight, followed by a slow and tender lament. Maybe a joyous rebirth or resurrection completes the cycle. First you need the story ...

(Tony Coult and Baz Kershaw, *Engineers of the Imagination: The Welfare State Handbook*)

Questions

- Can you apply any of these models to theatre you have read or seen?
- How might you use them in your own work?

Forms and devices

Whatever the overall style, the range of available dramatic storytelling devices is impressive. Many are exampled in the case studies, some are summarised above, a few more are listed below. Be bold, experiment and surprise yourselves.

A few more devices: Machine, distorting chronology – flashback, look to the future, fast/slow motion; sound montage; letter; thought tracking; tableau; monologue; mime; techniques of Epic Theatre; song; poetic language; taped or real sound effects; etc.

- *What can you add to this list?*

Rehearsal Methods and Techniques

'To develop my character I did a lot of hotseating ... I took a walk around his room and discovered he was a very neat person. I took a trip to the future with him to see what happened after the play.' (Student deviser)

Different rehearsal methods suit different styles of theatre. Those outlined below focus on practitioners and their methods. The account is necessarily brief. To explore in more depth consult *Further Reading* (p. 125).

Approaching character

Broadly speaking, you can think of character from two points of view, psychological truth or representation. In practice, you will probably end up with a mixture of both.

Naturalistic acting

To present a character the audience believes in, then you must believe in them too. One approach to creating belief is based on the work of *Konstantin Stanislavski*, a Russian theatre director (1856–1938). He developed 'The System' of actor training which encouraged the actor to find as realistic a performance as possible through a psychological approach. His concern was to create 'artistic truth' on stage. These exercises are based on a formula he derived from a lifetime's practice in the theatre. Much of what you know about your character won't be revealed explicitly in the performance, but on a subtle level the audience will recognise the depth and complexity of character. Naturalistic acting is sometimes a sustained sequence but can also be cut up episodes as in film.

▶ **Develop ideas in a notebook. The act of writing makes them concrete and you can return to them if you get lost.**

(*Where Stanislavski named exercises, they are given in italics.*)

1) Create the facts of your character's life – name, age, where they live, relations, etc. Create a background – first day at school, favourite book, an incident on a family holiday, etc.
2) With other devisers playing significant roles, improvise a) the most important moment in your character's life, b) the most painful farewell, and c) the most exciting meeting.
3) *Write as 'stories'* (see example form on p. 101).
4) *Emotion memory*: Identify the emotions your character experiences in the narrative. Choose the most important. Think back to a time when you felt the same emotion. Recall the circumstances, the colours and textures of the space, your feelings, the colour of the emotion, its shape, where you felt it in your body.
5) *Magic If*: 'If acts as a lever into the imagination' (Stanislavski). Imagine you are the character in their situation, 'What would I do *if*?'

6) *Method of physical actions*: Only use actions when you can identify an internal cause.
7) *Units and objectives*: Divide your play into scenes or units of action. Give your character a desire or objective.

What other improvisations can you think of that would help you develop narrative and character? Try them out.

Representative acting

This is based on close observation and accurate imitation. It results in a *demonstrative* style where characters are slightly larger than life. The emphasis is on type rather than psychological truth. It is often used in satire, political dramas and more crudely, pantomime. There is a strong visual emphasis on groupings and status. At any point relationships should be clear from how characters are positioned on stage. These ideas were developed by *Bertolt Brecht* (1898–1956) in the form of *Epic Theatre*. In Epic Theatre, 'everything hangs on the story' and all the elements of theatre service the telling of the story. The artifices of theatre are deliberately highlighted so that spectators are constantly reminded they are watching a play. Critical reasoning is more important than emotion.

1) *Gestus* means 'showing an attitude to people and situation through physical body language', which is very important in a style which emphasises visual storytelling. Identify your characters' attitudes towards an event in your piece, and create a tableau image or *gestic* image which communicates this visually. You could use this as a key moment in the scene – that which action moves towards and from.
2) *Observation and imitation*: Find someone you can study. Observe their way of walking and copy them. Listen to their speech habits and copy them. Observe any small habits and copy them. Apply to your character.
3) *As an actor, to maintain a distance, or objectivity, from your character*: Talk about your character in the third person as you enact the scene, 'he said', 'she sat'. Swap roles.
4) *For playing different roles*: Practise singing 'Jingle Bells' as The Sex Pistols, change to The Beatles and back. Repeat until you can transform from character to character instantaneously.

Surreal and Physical Theatre

Many of these forms derive from the work of *Antonin Artaud* (1898–1948), who wrote *Manifesto for a Theatre of Cruelty* to cleanse, shock and purify. He proposed a new relationship between actors and audience in an acting space where the audience sat in the middle of the action. He was interested in ritual; this was reflected in an acting style which was exaggerated and full of meaningful gesture. His staging ideas included giant puppets that mingled with the actors, richly coloured swathes of material blowing on stage, and strange new sounds played in the auditorium. *Peter Brook* (1925–), *Jerzy Grotowski* (1933–99) and *Steven Berkoff* (1937–) are contemporary practitioners who have built on and developed *Artaud's* ideas.

1) *Making the inanimate animate*: In groups of 4–7 create a) a blackberry bush with someone picking the blackberries; b) a flock of birds; c) someone walking through a rain cloud; d) an army approaching a house to arrest the inhabitant.
2) *Creating spaces,* using voice and body only: pairs enter as if in a) a dark cave; b) a cathedral; c) a library; d) a club.
3) *Creating nightmare states*: share dreams and choose one to improvise. Concentrate on mood and atmosphere. Use different levels; sound (percussion, choral voices, other); physically experiment with fast and slow motion; break chronology; limit your verbal text and use it poetically or in non-normal voices, etc.
4) *Characterisation*: base character on an animal and find new ways of moving.
5) *Emotional Wall (Grotowski)*: an immobile wall of torment seemingly impossible to break through. Breath initiates action and exemplifies emotion. Confront it using inhalation to physicalise the torment. Blow it away on out breath, blowing back from the wall. Repeat and experiment. Minor characters mirror major character for impact.

Forum, Image and Invisible Theatre

These are used by many contemporary theatre companies, particularly within Theatre in Education (TiE). These forms were developed by *Augusto Boal* (1931–) in Brazil to empower peasant people.

1) The subject of Boal's *Forum Theatre* is inequality in power relationships; spectators watch the action, then suggest ways

characters could have acted differently for a different outcome. They are invited on stage to enact their suggestion. Playing out possibilities on stage is a rehearsal for life, breaking the oppression shown in that situation.

2) *Image Theatre*: practice centres around making a physical image of an oppression or idea with people and/or objects and developing it, perhaps through interior monologues, to dialogues, to action. You might use this to develop ideas at the start of your process, or when you feel creatively blocked.

3) *Invisible Theatre*: planning a dramatic event in an ordinary place, e.g. a restaurant, the street, a train, where the audience think they are witnessing life. Try staging an argument in a café.

4) *Physical warm-up games*: to break down barriers in a group and find uncharacteristic attitudes of movement. *Boal* gives instructions for a vast range of exercises and performance possibilities in *Games for Actors and Non-Actors* (see *Further Reading,* p. 125).

Other sources of rehearsal techniques

Max Stafford Clark in *Letters to George* (see *Further Reading,* p. 125) documents a rehearsal process in which he effectively used playing cards and status exercises in the development of the play.

Trestle Theatre Company developed the practice of using 'tension states' for effective physical work in rehearsal and performance:

1. Physical and mental exhaustion – a severe hangover – difficult to move, unfocused and rambling.
2. Californian! Very cool, relaxed and laid back. No pressure, give and take. Unthreatening and fluid.
3. Neutral, unemotional. Just enough tension to get the job done.
4. The Director. Critical, interested and committed. Head led, precise, getting it right.
5. Optimist. Drawn towards things. A bit too curious. A bit too enthusiastic. The energy can be visible or restrained.
6. Pessimist. Negative and repelled by everything. A sense of phobia and paranoia. Unable to cope, stressed and pressurised.
7. Too much curiosity, too much repulsion. Rigor mortis sets in as mind and body are immobilised.

Keith Johnstone's Impro: This is an exciting source book full of ideas for rehearsals based on play and spontaneity.

Steven Berkoff's Metamorphosis: Berkoff originally published the text as a record of performance. However, descriptions of action and stage direction enable the exploration of a physical theatre style.

Voice: Voice warm-ups should be an important part of your devising rehearsals. Combine vocal and physical work to develop freedom and expressiveness. Start with yawning and sighing, sing songs you know together while skipping and running round the space. *Grease* is very singable. Enjoy using your voice freely and expressively. Cicely Berry, Patsy Rodenburg and Kristin Linklater have published excellent practical books for exploring and developing vocal potential (see p. 125).

Questions

- Perhaps reading through this chapter, you will have remembered rehearsal ideas or exercises you found effective. Note them in your journal.

- Can you see how you might develop some of these exercises for use in your rehearsals?

- How helpful might reading about practitioners' rehearsal practice be to you? How might you select exercises most appropriate to your group's work?

Glossary

Practitioners

See chapter 8 *Structuring Stories and Rehearsal Strategies* for more information.

Theatre Language

Commedia dell'arte Mask-based, artificial theatre form popular in Italy in the sixteenth and seventeenth centuries.

Farce Comedy in a slapstick style. See *Trestle Theatre's* case study, *Fool House* (pp. 21–30).

Form is often used to imply the obvious structure and shape of a piece, 'a three act', or 'episodic' play. The use may also be extended to describe devices, techniques and conventions used to make meaning as in 'direct address', 'monologue', or 'projected images'.

Forum Theatre and **Image Theatre** See *Boal* (pp. 118–119).

Genre and style are often used interchangeably. They mean forms of theatre with their own codes and conventions, e.g. Epic Theatre (p. 113, 117), Naturalism (p. 114, 116), Physical Theatre.

Gestus A theatre device. (See Brecht, p. 117).

Magic If see Stanislavski (p. 116).

Montage The techniques of placing disparate scenes next to each other and running them quickly to create a greater meaning than the sum of the parts. Coined by Brecht for his theatre practice.

Physical Theatre Emphasis on physical actions and gestures to express meaning, as opposed to the spoken text.

Promenade performance A play which is set on several different stages. The audience walk to the action.

Protagonist The main character/s in a play.

Story The action of an episode in devised theatre.

Tragedy see p. 000.

Technical terms

Gauze A cloth which is opaque when light is shone from in front, and transparent when light is shone from behind. Use it to create illusions.

Gel Coloured piece of plastic which is put front of the lens of a stage light to colour the beam.

Warm-Up and Rehearsal Games and Exercises

A tiny selection of those available – for fun, focus, discipline and developing skills

Energisers

Do you like your neighbour? A version of musical chairs. Chairs in circle. One too few for number of players. The object is not to be left in the middle. Ask sitters randomly, 'Do you like your neighbour?' If the answer is 'Yes', neighbours exchange; answer 'No', and everyone exchanges.

Fruit Bowl Another version of musical chairs. Arrange chairs as in *Do you like your neighbour?* Each player is named one of three fruits. The chairless person calls a fruit name, and those people change places. For *Fruit Bowl* everyone changes places. The caller rushes for a seat. Once the group have the hang of the game, different questions can be asked.

'Anyone who didn't brush their teeth today', etc. Forfeits and other more sophisticated rules can be built in.

Zip zap boing The principle is to send energy round and across a circle of players with energetic movements of voice and body. Players stand in a circle and with large gestures, send energy with the words 'zip', 'zap' and 'boing'. 'Zip' sends energy to the person next to you. 'Zap' sends the energy to someone across the room, and 'boing' changes the direction of the energy. You can't 'zap' a 'boing'. Play fast and energetically. Players who make mistakes are out.

Budge Pairs sit on chairs. One player has no chair. Cat chases mouse. To avoid being caught mouse says 'budge' and displaces a player from a chair. The displaced player becomes the cat, the cat becomes the mouse.

Trust exercises

Trust exercises often involve falling, lifting, rolling, blindfold and massage. They are about trusting yourself physically to the care of your group. They should always done with right mindedness and concentration; some music can support the process. They are well documented in Clive *Barker's Theatre Games* (see *Further Reading*, p. 125)

Exploring space

Five point exercise Facilitator picks five points on the stage. Four or five actors each position themselves at one. Then choose a route around, e.g. 5,1,3,2,4. They stand at the starting point and move at the same time to the next place. Accidents happen, people meet. Vary mood through different instructions, e.g. everyone looks at one person, or leaves looking to their last resting place. (source Toby Wilsher)

Building Groups

Nice and Nasty (p. 88) and **The Yes Game** (p. 26).

The Yes Game is an improvisation game which is about developing imagination, spontaneity and play. For a group, brainstorm situations – airport, bus, park, holiday, the street, etc. Pairs choose a starting situation and improvise. Work develops through saying 'Yes' literally or metaphorically, and enacting your own and each other's ideas. Make them as physical as possible so you move and travel. 'Help me push this trolley'. 'It's really heavy' 'Yes. It's full of lead'. 'We need a horse to pull it.' Etc. Each pair is on a journey together. There is no evidence. Pairs may interact if they cross each other's paths. The more you let your imaginations lead you, the more fun it will be. This is a game to return to when devising no longer seems fun. See Keith Johnstone's *Impro* (see *Further Reading*, p. 125) for more such games.

Physical actions

Tension States See *Trestle Theatre's* tension states p.119.

Building a Machine from a stimulus, one person expresses a physical and verbal response through a repeated gesture and phrase. One by one, other group members step in to build up a complex image. Use as a brainstorm. Developed it might end up in your piece.

Hiding and Hunted These are the games of your childhood – Sardines, Grandmother's Footsteps, Hide and Seek, Peter's Keys. If you can't remember them, look in Clive Barker's *Theatre Games* (see *Further Reading*).

Guardian Angel Walk the space. Don't talk or acknowledge others. Establish one person who is your enemy. Move as far away as you can. Choose another person and keep them in between you and your enemy. Develop variations.

Further Reading

On Devising and Rehearsal Activities

Clive Barker	*Theatre Games*	Methuen	1977
Belbin	'On the Workings of Groups' in *Understanding Organisations*	Penguin 4th Ed.	1993
Steven Berkoff	*Metamorphosis*	Amber Press	1989
Cicely Berry	*Voice and the Actor*	Harrap	1988
	The Actor and the Text	Virgin (Revised)	1993
Augusto Boal	*Games for Actors and Non-Actors*	Routledge	1992
Tony Coult and Baz Kershaw	*Engineers of the Imagination: The Welfare State Handbook*	Methuen	1990
Keith Johnstone	*Impro*	Methuen	1981
Kristin Linklater	*Freeing the Natural Voice*	Theatre Communication Group (USA)	1994
Shomit Mitter	*Systems of Rehearsal*	Routledge	1992
Alison Oddey	*Devising*	Routledge	1996
Thomas Richards	*At Home with Grotowski on Physical Actions*	Routledge	1995
Patsy Rodenburg	*The Actor Speaks: Voice and the Performer*	Methuen	1997
Viola Spolin	*Improvisation for the Theatre*	Northwestern University Press	1983
Max Stafford Clark	*Letters to George*	Nick Hern Books	1989

Approaches to Theatre

| Peter Brook | *The Empty Space* | Penguin | 1986 |
| Jerzy Grotowski | *Towards a Poor Theatre* | Methuen | 1985 |

Definitions

Terry Hodgson   *The Batsford Dictionary of*   Batsford   1988
                          Drama

Videos

Videos are available on application to the relevant companies:

Fool House   The Education Officer, Trestle Theatre Company, Birch Centre, Hill End Lane, St Albans, Herts AL4 0RA

70 Hill Lane   Education Officer, Improbable Theatre, c/o Battersea Arts Centre, Lavender Hill, London SW11 5TF

Animal Farm   Education Officer, Northern Stage Ensemble, Newcastle Playhouse, Barras Bridge, Haymarket, Newcastle upon Tyne NE1 7RH

Companies

These companies continue to devise exciting theatre and have active education departments. Write for details of work and performances. Many have set up Web sites. This small list is just a starting point.

Adzido Pan African Dance Company:	www.adzido-pan-african-dance-co.uk
DV8:	www.dv8.co.uk
Forced Entertainment:	www.forced.co.uk
Frantic Assembly:	www.franticassembly.co.uk
Graeae (drama and special needs):	Email: graeae@dircon.co.uk
GYPT (Greenwich and Lewisham Young People's Theatre, TiE):	Email: gypt@diron.co.uk
Improbable Theatre:	c/o Battersea Arts Centre, Lavender Hill, London SW11 5TF. www.improbable.co.uk
Nitro (formerly Black Theatre Co-op) (Black performing arts company):	www.nitro.co.uk

Northern Stage Ensemble: Newcastle Playouse, Barras Bridge, Haymarket, Newcastle upon Tyne, NE1 7RH.
www.northernstage.co.uk

Passe-Partout: Education, 13 Stanford Avenue, Brighton BN1 6AD
Email: enqs@passe-partout.demon.co.uk

Shared Experience: www.setheatre.co.uk

Steven Berkoff: www.east-productions.demon.co.uk

Strathcona (drama and special needs):   Email: stc@strathco.demon.co.uk

Theatre de Complicite: Education, Theatre de Complicite, 20–24 Eden Grove, London N7 8ED.
Email: email@complicite.co.uk

Volcano Theatre: 176 Hanover Street, Swansea SA1 6BP
www.volcanotheatre.co.uk

Welfare State International: The Ellers, Ulverston, Cumbria LA12 1AA.
www.welfare-state.org